2:54pm
February 24, 2025
From the desk of Tim Castleman

I've just completed the final read through of the Funnel Hacking Live Las Vegas notes. Page 146 marks the end of covering all 10 years of Funnel Hacking Live.

From a room that could barely hold 600 people to ballrooms that couldn't contain the energy from over 5000 thousand funnel hackers. The creation of the Two Comma Club award, to the domination of funnels and software to help everyday entrepreneurs like you. ClickFunnels, Russell & Todd have changed the lives of millions of people in the past 10 years.

This final Funnel Hacking Live marks a season of growth and change.

[Prime Mover](#) will be the foundation for Russell moving forward, while Todd & his amazing team will continue to improve and expand [ClickFunnels](#), with the goal of making it THE solution for businesses online.

It's been a privilege and honor to share our insights and recap these past 10 years but nothing happens in a vacuum. I want to thank Russell Brunson for inviting me to the first event in Las Vegas a decade ago. He doesn't know it, but this event saved my life more than once during a very dark time in my life and gave me something to look forward to when all appeared lost.

I also want to thank Myles Clifford, the unseen hero from FHL who made the events run so smoothly and working with ClickFunnels a joy. He always made sure we had a spot in the room and whatever we needed to provide you with the best recap & summary possible.

I want to thank the true star of these notes, Sue Antinoro, who was the backbone of making sure we capture every speaker of the event. These notes are a result of her dedication and hard work to translate everything seen from the stage to actionable information for you, the reader.

A special thanks to the Amazing Ava who spends days combing over the notes after the event to ensure everything is understandable, properly linked and readable for everyone's benefit.

Finally, I can never forget you dear reader. Without your trust in what we do and giving us the space to work (by buying the presale and giving us a few weeks to deliver the notes), I would be nothing.

The notes were a crazy idea I had on the way to a conference years ago that turned into a simple little business that changed my life and let me do something I can be extremely proud of for the rest of my life.

Your kind words, encouragement, and support gave me hope and served as a reminder that good still exists in this world. I have never taken you for granted and doing these notes has been a pleasure and a privilege for the past decade.

Like Russell, I'm always in search of my next adventure and I believe I've found it in the [Prime Mover](#) program. Although I've been to every FHL, this year was the first time I felt compelled to join the "big offer" (PRIME MOVER) at the end of the event.

Afterall, 2,678 millionaires can't be wrong and it's clear to me that Russell Brunson has the training, track record, support team, and infrastructure to make a few more ;) I hope in record time you and I are on the stage together celebrating the success of what is about to come.

2025 can be just another year or it can be THE YEAR of change for you.

I'm jumping in with both feet, and I hope to see you in the PRIME MOVER program. If you'd like to "look over my shoulder" as I work through PRIME MOVER and on business, reach out to me personally at contacttimcastleman@gmail.com.

In closing I just want to say the following, from the bottom of my heart:

THANK YOU   **THANK YOU**   **THANK YOU**

Tim Castleman

Russell Brunson

"The mass of men lead lives of quiet desperation." - Henry David Thoreau

Here's another one of my favorites quotes:

"The two most important day is your life are the day you were born and the day you find out why." - Mark Twain

You are going to be learning how to change the world and you'll learn how to change your world first. We've been doing this event now for a decade. We just wanted to build some software and you guys just kept showing up. During year two, 1,200 people came and the next year it was up to 3,500. This year we have over 5,000 people in the room.

For most people, the first time they come into this world, it's very scary. How many of you came here with a little fear in your heart? Entrepreneurship is a scary thing the first time.

For me, I was scared to death. But I felt this weird pull - it's called the call to contribution. Every time an opportunity shows up, it's scary. I always have this fear that no one will show up. You guys are here which makes me so happy. I found this quote which is part of the introduction of the Funnel Hacking documentary:

"Everyone is afraid the first time."

If you continue, you are one of the 1% crazies - welcome home!

You are in the 1% crazy room and you are the people we have been called to serve.

This morning I want to talk about your calling and where you might be on this journey. Some of you are new, and some have been earning $10 million a year, so everyone is at a different part in their journey.

The first thing I want to talk about is when you are starting any journey, one of the biggest mistakes people make is they start without any direction. For me, I had some kind of desire. I think those who can figure out what their purpose is, can be more successful early.

So what is your definite purpose? Some people will say they want to start a business, but a definite purpose is more specific.

I remember I was in the 8th grade and my dad wanted me to go to wrestling practice. I wasn't that into it at the time. There was no purpose and I was just going through the motions. There were two guys in the finals for the state tournament and we were sitting in the audience. There was a guy who went out there and won the match. I saw him getting his hand raised after he won, and I knew that's what I wanted.

As soon as I had a purpose to be the state champion, everything else disappeared from me. That's how bad you have to want the thing you are going after.

For the business, I wanted to make money but there was never any purpose. Then this guy John Reese launched a course and made $1M in an 18 hour window. I remember seeing that and telling myself that's what I wanted to do.

Later on in my business, I started making money. After you start making a lot of money, it's not as fulfilling as you think. I started looking at other people like Tony Robbins and my focus shifted to changing the lives of others.

As a wrestler, my favorite feeling was when my hand was raised after winning. A few years ago, my boys started wrestling and one of my sons said he didn't want to wrestle. I encouraged him but he kept losing matches. He was mad and defeated and during the entire season he kept losing.

Finally at the last match, I prayed he'd get some success. He won and got his hand raised and I remembered that felt so much more than getting my own hand raised. So when you can change someone else's life, that is the best feeling.

For most of you, the Hero's Journey is a big framework. The first thing is where you are starting out in the ordinary world. If you think about Lord of the Rings, Frodo started out in the shire to head out and start his adventure.

My guess is, before you came into this world, you lived in the ordinary world. Then you felt this call to contribution.

Next, the hero starts on the hero's journey, which is always moving toward your purpose. There's 3 tiers on your purposes. Simon Sinek talks about this in his book,

Start With Why:

1. What
2. How
3. Why

The goal of the why is what pushes you to keep going. I always struggled with the why part of it for a long time. As I was preparing for this presentation, all of a sudden I had something come into my head. I know what my why is and I'm going to give you a tool to figure it out.

Your why is two "Who's" - the first is you. Who do you want to become? What does your future self look like? That's why we surround ourselves with mentors.

In every hero's journey there is a second journey that the audience isn't aware of. The second journey is one of transformation. Who does the character become? Apollo Creed beat Rocky in the first movie. But who does Rocky become in that movie?

That's how you change the world. You change yourself, then more people start coming to you.

The second "Who" is who are you called to serve?

The first time I got into this business, I felt like God tricked me. He gives you this desire for money. Then we start out on this journey and, in any journey if you follow the hero's journey to the end, the last step is when he finds the secret and returns with the elixir and gives it to people.

When you come back to your customer, that's where your business journey starts.

At our third FHL, we did a presentation called One Funnel Away. On Saturday, I'm going to do a presentation called One Funnel Away Part 2, showing all the ups and downs. I think about the reasons why we go on this journey, going through all these ups and downs. It's hard sometimes, and we get lessons on pain, trials and tribulations. The reason is that we get stronger and we realize the person we are serving is you five years ago.

It's the thing that makes you worthy of the calling. That's why it's important to go through these things. Last year was hard and there's some insane momentum going on in ClickFunnels right now.

You wake up in the morning and you're tired, but you see your future self and your vision. Number two, you know you have to figure out how you are going to serve those people. Those are the only two things that get me up in the morning. Think about those two things, then the burden gets light. It gets fun and exciting.

The next thing that happens in the hero's journey is called the refusal of the call. You say to yourself "I can't do that because I'm not worthy." I talk too fast. I remember I was walking out during rehearsals and I stumbled out because I'd taken a breath of the smoke. Note to self - take a deep breath first before you walk through the smoke.

Throughout this weekend, you are going to hear this over and over again. When those things happen, maybe you think this speaker is speaking to you. Someone is going to speak to your heart and you are going to hear it.

Dan Kennedy talked yesterday about B2B marketing. In any room, there's a ⅓ of the room who are thinking that something isn't right here. They are waiting for the radical to show up. I asked him why don't those people step up and be the radical. It's because of the refusal of the call. That call must be made up in your head. I have a strong belief that those desires are put there by God.

I struggled in school, and barely graduated college but God put it in my heart about this funnel thing. I showed up and kept following up.

I remember the first time I did an event, we bought radio ads, rented the Holiday Inn, and we were going to the change the world. 100 people said they were going to come. Two people showed up and one person sat in the front row and one in the back. This was 20 years ago. No one wanted a funnel 20 years ago.

The reason why any of you care about this was I kept talking about it over and over. Eventually a decade later I met Todd. Then more and more people showed up. For you, it's the same thing. You'll keep talking about it and no one will show up. God's testing you and if you care more about the mission, you'll succeed.

After the calling happens, you'll hear the refusal of the call.

Steven Pressfield wrote Turning Pro and [The War of Art](The War of Art), where he talks about resistance in this book. It happens over and over. He said the things that really good writers understand is the writing part is not hard, it's the sitting down to do it. The hard part is not building the funnel, it's sitting down to do it.

So I thought I'm going to do a time study and see what it looks like. The next day, the alarm goes off, I hit the snooze button. Resistance is already starting. Have you done the time test yet? You'll realize how much the resistance pops up.

If you read Turning Pro, it's about stopping acting like an amateur and stepping into your calling. What does a pro do differently? They show up differently.

We have to decide "Yes I'm doing this" and we are going to move forward towards this calling.

After we make this decision, the next step is when the guide shows up. He doesn't show up initially, you have to do the steps first. Faith is taking that first step into the part. It's like stepping through the fog.

Rocky decides to box and Mickey shows up. Frodo decides to do the thing and Gandalf shows up. The guide gives the hero a map to achieve the purpose. One of the biggest mistakes is thinking now that we have the plan everything will be easy.

If you want to become something, there's always conflict. You get the map and it's up to you to start walking. You're not fully aware of what's going to happen. You'll leave this weekend, get home and you'll get hit with resistance.

The game is getting back up (think of Rocky V). Even though the guide gives you the plan, you gotta be ready for that journey. There will be ups and downs, but you need to be ready.

One day I was thinking about this idea. How many of you have heard people say they had an idea of something that's been invented? Who is willing to actually execute on this idea? I believe God starts with little ideas to test. He gave me the idea for the potato fun and Zip Brander. I was a good steward of executing ideas. Eventually 10 years later he gave me the idea of ClickFunnels.

I think a lot of you are waiting for the ClickFunnels idea. When you get the small ideas, you just do it. Go forward and see what happens. If no one buys anything, no one knows. That's not embarrassing because no one saw it. There's so much fear about launching, but just do it.

There's two driving forces: there's faith and fear. Most of us by default pick one or the other. In "Outwitting the Devil", Napoleon Hill calls them drifters. They choose fear, fear shuts them down and hope someone else takes it on. The other one is faith, and I call those people The Driven. Those are the ones who move forward in faith.

There's three types of faith you have to have to be successful.

1. Faith in the purpose - because I believe these ideas come from God, I'm just going to move forward. If you don't believe this came from outside of yourself, it's so easy to back out.

2. Faith in the guide - one of the most frustrating conversations I have is when a coaching student doesn't want to take my advice because of some podcaster. You have to pick one map, put on blinders and focus.

    I remember I was in the airport once, and I saw this guy running at me. He's a young kid and he asked me what advice would you have now? He told me he's studying all these things and I told him to get one mentor. He liked real estate, and I told him to unsubscribe from my lists and focus on a real estate person for advice.

    So pick one mentor, put on blinders and focus. I want to help people to get to the finish line and if it's not me, that's fine. Just go.

3. Lastly, you need to have faith in you. If you are not in a spot where you have faith in yourself, that's ok. You will earn that faith by doing it. When I was growing up in school, I thought I was dumb. I struggled in school, graduated with a 2.3 GPA and it wasn't until I launched my business where they eventually liked my ideas. It turns out I'm not actually dumb but it took me a little while. So if you don't trust yourself yet, that's okay. The key is to start going down the path and you'll get that faith in yourself during the journey.

How To Get Anything You Want by Elsie Lincoln Benedict

I started buying all the books and Napoleon Hill was talking about this woman back in 1910. This woman was filling up these stadiums. At the time there weren't a lot of women authors. She would do these private seminars and her company was the opportunity. Eventually I found a set of her books, and then she had another book set called "Brainology" and it was twice as many books. I think I was missing 3-4 books and we are scouring every site to find them.

Then we launched Secrets of Success and told the story. Inside the community, we had members find the books for us and now we are republishing them all for the community.

Now if you do all this you'll believe in yourself and you can start changing other's lives. If you are willing to step into that calling, you'll be able to make money but you'll also be able to feel what it's like to change someone's life. This is a lifestyle where you are changing people's lives and it'll change everything for you.

One day years ago, Dave Woodward and I were talking about the ripple effect. There's us and 300 employees, but all of those employees have families. At the time we had 70,000 customers. But all of those, each of them have spouses and kids and it's changing their lives. Plus they also had employees, and they are also serving someone. Kaelin Poulin had millions on her email list for example.

People are coming here from all around the world. They will leave empowered and the ripple effect will literally change the world. I want you to think that way. Shift from how to make money to thinking about the ripple effect, and someday when this whole thing is done, think about all the people who will tell you how you changed their life. How cool will that be some day?

If you look at this event, everything fits into a couple of pillars. To be successful you have to have a really good offer. I call it a Level 10 offer. If you have that, people will be sprinting to the back of the room or running to their credit card to buy. The first part of this conference is about offers.

After that, you have to understand how to have a presentation to sell that offer. We'll talk about how to create a one to many presentation.

Day number three we'll go deeper into funnels.

For me this journey started a lot earlier. In 2005, I was 20 years old. I bought ClickDotCom.com and started building. We called them sales flows instead of funnels at the time. This was the first version of ClickFunnels that we tried to build. A few years later, everything collapsed for us and we had to lay off a bunch of employees. I remember Tony Robbins saying that on people's deathbeds, they say that the thing they thought was the worst thing turned out to be the best thing.

So I reset my course and was trying to figure out what to do. I was on Flippa.com and I found this email/text responder site. I bought the company and thought I'd rebrand Champion Sound for a variety of businesses. It turned out it was coded in Ruby on

Rails, and no one knew how to code it. Finally, after four weeks of trying to get it to work, we shut it down.

As I was leaving the office, I remember feeling a weird impression. I believe it was from God and it said to email my list to see if there was a Ruby on Rails developer. So I sent the email out and a few hours later, I got a response from a guy saying he could help. I sent him the log in details and the next day he'd fixed all the bugs and changed some things up. Of course, that person was Todd Dickerson. He came into our world when everything was falling apart and for the first year he showed up and didn't ask for any money.

I remember looking over his shoulder and he had all these job offers that were paying a lot. He told me he didn't want a job, he just wanted to make cool stuff. But I knew I had to pay him something and fast forward six months later, I paid him $100,000 a year. One day he was flying out to Boise to work on a project, and that morning LeadPages had just gotten $5M in funding. Todd told me he could build another LeadPages today.

That started the conversation and all this stuff we'd been thinking of for years. At the time we had a domain called ClickFusion. Todd said that domain was cursed and we had to find another one, so we bought ClickFunnels instead. We were brainstorming about the future and he said to me that he didn't want to do it as one of my employees, but instead as a partner. So I agreed and over a decade later, the two greatest decisions I've made are marrying my wife Collette, and the second was making Todd my business partner.

Todd - No one told me that it was impossible, and I didn't know the full backstory. How many of you have been told that your dreams are impossible? Don't listen to it, because you can do it.

I had built a pretty successful side business and I had read the 4 Hour Workweek, so when ClickFunnels was set up, I had decided I wanted to have more impact. When your email came in, it was divine timing.

On Sept. 23, 2014 we officially launched ClickFunnels.

Our Mission

To free all entrepreneurs (the dreamers and the doers) so you can focus on changing the lives of the people that you've been called to serve.

Since ClickFunnels started, we've had:

- $11,379,117,412 billion in sales processed (doesn't include anything off platform)
- 2,689 Two Comma Club winners
- 388 Two Comma Club X winners
- 125 Two Comma Club C winners
- 11 "Two Heart" winners - people who have donated $1M to charity
- The Three Comma Club Award - we reached that level ourselves and I want to give all of you the next tier to strive towards.

We've also had some new branding changes recently. For the last 2 years, we feel like we needed to freshen stuff up. It was hard for me to be okay with this, but most big companies have logos that have changed over time. So I was willing to entertain the thought of this, and we spent 8-9 months going through the process. We hired a big branding company to help us with this process.

It's more than a logo, it's also a fundamental update on how we view our software in the future. We kept thinking about how we do funnels. It's not just your landing page, you take your workflow and you also do that in your community and in your stores.

Andy Elliott

Chase the man, not the money. The money will come when you become who you are supposed to become.

I come to you today as a husband, someone that was laughed at my whole life. I still wear the shortest shorts in the world because I like making people laugh. I want to train today like I've never trained before. Who here came here to change your life? That chair you are sitting in is a hundred million dollar chair. Today I'm going to share a $100M idea with you.

Most people are never present. When I sat in your chair in 2019, I made a decision that changed my life. You have to trust and have faith. Some of you take this lightly. The reason why I get so passionate is I know what that chair is worth now. I sat there and no one knew me. I had no business. I am a car salesman, which is at the bottom of the food chain.

My dad left when I was two, and he was a coward. He never stood for anything. Some of you know who you don't want to be. This is an opportunity for me to give you your mind and soul. I used to be average, fat and never helped anyone. I used to be an average father and an average husband. I used to never help anyone. All of that can change in an instant.

If you listen to me, you can change your life in the next hour. I was a fool, but I know how to learn. But I fell in love with learning. I want to build the greatest leaders that have been built on the planet. I want you to become rich and I want you to have a rich life. Do you want to be a great father? So many men chasing business are destroying their families. They think you have to sacrifice things.

So you want money, but you ignore your family. Or you are close to your wife but you are not there to take your son from boyhood to manhood. Who believes they can be worth $100M? Look how many people don't have their hands up.

Today is day one of your success. I want you to feel it and be hungry. I want it to be screaming inside of you. I want to see if you are willing to be made a fool. Yes you are going to be made fun of and be misunderstood. In 2014, I'm in the car business and I wanted to train my salespeople. So I recorded ten videos teaching how to overcome people's objections when buying a car. I didn't know anything about the internet. The only thing I knew was internet leads.

I tell my wife I need to record these ten videos so my salespeople could watch. She puts them on YouTube. I don't even know what YouTube is. Who here feels insecure when it comes to the camera? That's me, I'm an introvert. If you want to create influence you are going to build a brand. If you want to change people's lives, you need a brand.

Then in 2019, my wife told me that those videos had hundreds of thousands of views. Many comments were negative but there were also many that said I changed their life. I didn't know what to think of it, but I'd been hated on my whole life. Can you take the hate? **When you change someone's life they send you messages in the DMs. When people hate, they live in the comments section.**

No one in my bloodline has helped anyone change their life. I felt like I was always missing something. All the crap I'd been through was getting me ready and something was going to happen. I'm here to tell you that if you listen to me, if you pray to get rich, you'll get big problems. If you want to have a big life, you'll have big problems. You say you want a big life, but do you really?

I was that hater for a long time. I didn't believe that lives existed for people like us. And it's not even that hard to get.

I married a Mexican woman, who is very direct. One day I told her I was on my way home. I was actually working a deal. She was heating the food up, and that night she'd say something that would break my heart. It made me feel like I'd let everyone down. I had three beautiful kids. She told me that she and the kids had learned to live life without me. When I was home, my mind was at work.

Scarcity has been beaten into me as a kid. Being one dimensional is what I see around the world. People don't believe they can lead a big team, be close to God, have a great marriage, etc. That night my wife was drawing a line. Was I going to play the victim or reinvent my life?

I went into the garage, worked out for 4 hours. I was fat at the time. When I met my wife, I was 26 and she was 24. When she told me she and the kids were learning to live without me, I knew that she loved me more than anything else. So many of us could be better in this room. But we don't have anyone telling us the truth and pushing us.

Then she reached over and grabbed my love handle. It felt like spiders crawling up my back. She knew the way I took care of myself is the way I take care of everything in my life. Woman, many of you put yourself last. When you take care of yourself, you become the bloodline breaker in your family as a female. A great woman will tell her man when he's slipping.

There's this thing I see happen to men in their 40s. He's either going to get another 40 years or he dies. I needed this from her. I shaved my head as I wanted to see a different person as fast as possible. I needed motivation.

I went online, and it was my first time online. I typed in "motivation" and Google sent me a youtube video of Tony Robbins. I started watching and within minutes I'm thinking differently. For the first time in my life I wanted to be a different person. I watched the next one as fast as I could. I learned my mind isn't my friend. The greatest gift you can give yourself is working on you.

Tony Robbins made an offer. This was November 2019. **Who here has a specialized skill? People will pay you for that information to get somewhere faster.** I didn't believe it but what if it was true? I watched this video with Dean Graziosi, Russell Brunson and Tony Robbins. I was good at sales and I remember staring at the computer screen. I was thinking if I was worth it and this was stupid.

Then, I decided to bet on myself. I was broken that night and I needed a change. I was making $2M a year in 2019 and I quit my job when I bought that course. For 21 years I was the GOAT at selling cars, but I never changed anyone's life.

I almost went to jail, ran with the wrong people and wasn't always a good husband to my wife. I had so many reasons why I shouldn't have clicked that buy button. My wife wants to see her man rise. She knew there was a guy inside to create greatness. When I bought that course, I quit my job, and studied the KBB training course for the next 30 days.

After training for 28 days, I'd reinvented myself. My eyes changed color and I was ready for war but I was still broken. I thought I'd changed but this led me to believe that I hadn't yet. There was a 30 day money back guarantee. Some of you, you need someone like my wife to be next to you when you have these moments.

My wife told me, you don't want your students to refund their money. How would you like that? But yet, you want a refund from this program? She's the truth teller in my corner. **I learned that if you want money, you have to devalue it.**

As embarrassing as that moment was, I started to understand what our future would be like. I started going all in on shooting content.

I'm a psycho-competitor. I love what I do. I started shooting content and I knew that Google had served me a video that sent me to Tony Robbins. **I typed in "motivation" and Google is telling you "People also searched".**

I was in the automotive industry so I went to Google and typed in "car sales training". If you type that in, it'll pull up my YouTube videos. I would go on a journey to type that in and it would say "people also searched". I'd make videos every day on those other titles. That was step 1. Everyone needs to know who you are, how they can get a hold of you and how great you are.

If you want to be the best, it's time to build both paid and organic marketing. How much easier is it for the sales team to close people when your potential buyers have watched your videos?

Step 2 - Has anyone seen Gary Vee's community? One day I'm watching him back in 2020 and I'm shooting free long form videos every day. The only people liking these were my wife. So don't stop - it takes time.

I told her that Gary Vee put his cell phone number on the internet. Because I'm an idiot, I thought it was his cellphone. Imperfect action beats no action every day. I got on my next video and I'd say, if this video has helped you, shoot me a text and I put my number up there. I told them I had their back for life.

I had no idea what would happen three years later. I had put my cell phone number in 4,000 videos. The craziest thing started to happen. People were texting me all the time. I was inspired to teach sales training.

I soon found out that you can reinvent yourself every day. Every day, my team gets a new leader. You guys can roll this way too. Do you want your team to outgrow you? Do you want your wife to outgrow you? Do you want your parents to outgrow you? No, you want them to be constantly changing. You want to keep growing and growing.

If you are going to make it big, you can be the best in business but you'll never compete if they have a better personal life than you do. This isn't taught anymore. You want to be on fire and kill it? You need to recreate every day.

After 21 years, finally I looked in the mirror and I decided I'm taking my family with me. If they don't like my family they will not be my customers. We lived in Oklahoma and a million dollar house was our dream house. My wife, when she saw how I changed, told me we were selling the house.

You need to give up your old life if you want to go all in. Do you want to be a GOAT? If you do, quit thinking so small. A lot of you say if your wife sold your house, you sold your kids on the dream.

I still hadn't sold anything yet. My life had changed faster in 3 months than it did in 15 years. For the first time in my life, my wife believed in me. She knew her husband would spend a lot of money on mentors. I wanted to know how everything worked. The devil doesn't want you to work on yourself so you could remain average your whole life.

We drove $1,500 cars, sold our house and slept on mattresses on the floor. We fell in love with each other all over again. If you want to do something that's never been done, you need to change your whole life.

If you want a good life, that's okay. But those chairs are $100M chairs. What do you see? "I'm too old." "I bought that one course". Today I have this crazy life, because everything Russell is teaching you this weekend, is selling one to many.

For the next year after we sold the house, I had nothing to sell. I finally listened to what Russell said. You need a funnel and you need an offer. So I made this new YouTube training on how to make $100K in sales.

I always wanted to teach people and I didn't know you could get paid for it. I put it into a 21 video training that I sold for $299. I made the video, went to sleep, woke up the next morning with $150K in my bank account. For the first time in my life, I saw that it was working.

You all have something here, that's called a leash. You are all on a leash and you need to cut it. Just cut it! What if it doesn't happen fast? It'll happen. You'll never know if you don't cut the leash.

Prove them right or wrong, you decide. I blow my voice out non stop because I know it's possible. What do you think God wants? He's asking you to rise up and believe in yourself.

Two years after that course was launched, I'd built my team. I live in Arizona and we have 100 people on my team. All we talk about is saving souls and changing lives. We don't even have a revenue board. We replaced it with transformation. We know what to do. You have the specialized skill and people will pay.

In the next couple of years, if you've ever wanted to be great, you make a decision today and I promise you, from now until the end of this event, you'll brainwash yourself. You'll think about the things you need to start doing. You are the product.

You have someone inside of you that the world has never met. If people want to play small, that's fine but what do you feel? Do you feel a tugging? When I bought that first course, and it changed my life I knew I'd keep learning until I'd die. Winners always get a ROI. Losers always ask "what if it doesn't work?"

My team and I would annihilate the automotive industry. In the beginning you go niche, then we went wide. Today we train over 10,000 companies. All because I believed in myself. My wife sold our house to back me. I knew she believed in me, but it took me to stand up.

We went viral on social media. If you are not doing it, you're an idiot. Social media is free. Make it, don't consume it. Can you inspire anyone? What if you only helped one person, would it be worth it? What if I told you that some of you in this room would change hundreds of millions of lives?

I was made fun of as a kid. I always wanted to make a lot of money so I would have choices. I stuttered until I was 18. When I met my wife it was the first time someone believed in me. Now, haters motivate me. I don't care what anyone says.

An individual can be beat, but a team can't be beat. If you want to make history you are going to need a team. After 18 years, most people are sleeping in the same bed but are miles apart. Not in my home.

Some of my team is here with me today. Tommy was a drug addict for 16 years. His wife pulled a needle out of his arm, found him dead and brought him back to life. The devil wants you to think you are counted out. This coaching, this reason why you are here is something you can sell one to many.

Tommy bought my training course and now he's with me on my team. When he came to one of my first events, he would show up and I told him if he got clean, you can come back and I'll give you a job. Now he's a 7 figure earner for my company. This isn't about me.

What about the people's lives that you change in your own company? Is it worth it? Don't think small.

For everyone one of you, I wish God would let me show you guys what your life will look like on the other side of all these decisions that are running through your head. This is how your kids will look at you, this is the influence you are making.

If I hadn't hit "click" when I was 40, I wouldn't be here. Now that I know it's possible I want you to think about being a car salesperson for 21 years…lost people don't know they are lost. If I could talk to anyone who's been the least likely to make it, now's the time. There's a key to success.

Performance - you have to work harder than anyone has ever worked. It's hard but worth it.

Knowledge - you must find mentors and pay them to train you.

God loves all of you so much. You'll see how your journey will align. The right people will show up. Immerse in this and become obsessed with it. If you have a family, make sure you take them with you.

McCall Jones
Charisma Hacking

Russell Brunson is the Bob Ross of selling. And you are all dropping secrets, transitioning from teaching, getting to the offer and then you get to the pitch. There's no eye contact being made and your presentation ends. You check Stripe and there's only a trickle of sales. You think to yourself you followed the steps. You think this product could change lives but why aren't they buying?

Kristen and Sylvia help Shopify sellers. Monday - Thursday they spend all their money on ads. Friday comes, the audience shows up and they go crazy for the info but they wouldn't buy. They started tweaking slides and asked me to hop on a call with them.

After we made tweaks they closed 20% and they bought the upsells. Tonight they are collecting their 2CC award. So what changed?

The secret was they knew how to take the most boring part of the sales presentation and make it the most exciting. If you can say the right things in the right way, you can sell like Russell.

We are going to focus on one part of the sales presentation. This is where we move from teaching to selling. We're going to fix it in 3 easy steps.

1. Cookie-ify
2. Timeline-ify - what to say
3. Charisma-ify - how to say it

Cookie-ify

- A product is a single item
- An offer is items packaged together to get a result

For example - protein powder vs powder plus coaching for weight loss

Just because you have an offer doesn't mean you have a good offer. If you take a bunch of stuff and bundle it, it might make you seem worse. This is a yard sale mistake.

For example, you changed your offer to protein powder and a logo redesign. Even if a logo design is more valuable on paper, people will pay 10X more for results than they will for products.

The people who make this mistake are the smartest people with the most knowledge.

For example Bob teaches social media marketing. He knows a lot about a lot of things. Everytime he launches a new offer, he'll be tempted to include his investing course for entrepreneurs. But it's a trap.

3 Rules To Follow

1. Just because it's valuable doesn't mean it belongs in your offer
2. Just because you spent a long time building it doesn't mean its belongs in your offer
3. Just because people paid $ for it elsewhere doesn't mean it belongs in your offer

If You Give A Mouse A Cookie - this is the original offer playbook

The story goes, that if you give a mouse a cookie, he's going to ask for a glass of milk, etc. In the book, every problem Mr. Mouse has is solved. One problem creates the next one, but he's completely taken care of.

For example, if he wants to lose weight, you give him protein powders. If you give him protein powders, he's going to need a recipe. Then he'll need a workout plan, and a community to keep him motivated.

For every problem you'll add things to your offer to solve that problem.

Watch how Russell does it during his presentations.

You have the training. Some people get stuck on X, so you need copy to be successful.

When you build a mouse cookie offer, every item builds on each other to build a result. Everything in the path must be solved in your offer.

If you don't know how to solve all the problems that's okay because not everything in your offer needs to come from you.

Kelsey trains next level athletes. If people need more energy during games she solves it with her own problems.

But then someone says they need to learn to jump higher - she doesn't know how to solve this. Rather than learning, she partnered with a fitness trainer to solve the problem.

If you present your offer in the wrong way your audience will still drag their feet.

Timeline-ify

Instead of dumping everything on them we present in the order that our customers face their problems on their path. Once you have solution #1, you'll need solution #2. Once you have solution #2, you'll need solution #3, etc.

- Funnel
- Funnel design course
- Copy
- Traffic

They will see themselves crossing the finish line with your help. This is an easy way to hijack their subconscious.

Think of the movie, Crazy Stupid Love. In that movie, Ryan Gosling teaches Steve Carell the right things to say to pick up women. He tries but it goes wrong.

Rusell makes it look so easy because he's perfected the right way to talk about his offers. He also controls the energy in the room.

There are two tactics with charisma hacking:

- Customer's problems in a way that takes them from overlooked to feeling seen
- Your own success from feeling overwhelmed to action

When you are writing copy, you put your customer's pain language all over the page. But on video, it's different.

There are 3 charisma trust styles and each talks about pain in different ways:

1. Steady
2. Fix
3. Mirror

One will come naturally to you. The other will repel your customers

- Steady
    - You are soft and empathetic.
    - You focus on emotions.
    - Like Vishen Lakhiani from MindValley.

- Fix
    - Action readers
    - Very matter of fact
    - They say things like "You may be doing X"
    - Like Alex Hormozi

- Mirror
    - Mind readers
    - Expressive and focus on thoughts
    - They say "You may be thinking" and act it out
    - Like Russell Brunson

Find real life situations where you needed someone to trust you. Were you behaving like a steady, a fixer, or like a mirror?

How To Talk About Your Own Success

- Some people slowly shrink into insecurity when they talk about their own success
- Some people are so full of themselves

3 Charisma Authority Styles

Each has different attributes. They do different things with hands and language and each talks about their success in different ways.

1. Light
2. Life
3. Lead

One of these will come naturally to you.

- Light
    - They say "trust the path" it worked for them and it will work for you
    - Like Russell Brunson
    - 10% of people are light

- Lift
    - They say "trust yourself"
    - There are people like you who have succeeded so why not you
    - Like Dean Graziosi
    - 40% of people are lift

- Lead
    - They say "trust me", I know how to get this result, so why do it alone
    - An assertive motivator
    - Like Alex Hormozi
    - 50% of people are lead

The other styles will sabotage. How to know which ones to use? Find situations when you needed to convince a friend you knew what to do. Which were you?

Use this key to reverse engineer:

If you are Light - and you use lead, you'll appear aggressive
If you are Lift - you'll appear aggressive and abandoning people
If you are Lead - you'll appear abandoning and uncertain

They will see your true expertise and not your bravado and are more likely to buy on the spot.

At my first FHL in 2020, Russell said, you have something that will change someone's life. It's your moral responsibility to give it to them. He didn't say you should sell it to make money.

I got home and I was on fire. As reality set in, I knew there were thousands of people teaching people on how to be confident on camera. I started to panic and think who am I to compete with them? As a new business owner, I went to my sister in law who had a funnel design course. I asked how do you stand out?

She showed me her course vs a competitor's course. When they completed the competitors course, they got a certificate in the mail. In her course, module 8 was to sell your first design. Her students were making money before they finished the course. This is the difference between information and transformation.

Transformations are judged by what someone achieves by the end. Only one takes someone from pain and gives them skills. It's your responsibility to learn how to sell it. There are people who need you and they are surrounded by information. They are waiting for your mouse and cookie offer.

Myron Golden

Creating wealth can be close to effortless. The struggle is not real, it's imagined. You can create whatever level of wealth you want if you understand how it works.

Why do the rich get richer and the poor get poorer? The poor get poorer because they don't understand how financial life works.

Everyone has resources. You have an asset and it is a limited depreciating asset. That is time. You've been told that the key to getting money is to exchange time for money. So you trade your time for money.

Time is limited and one of the reasons you are struggling is because as long as your revenue generation is tied to time, the money you can get will always be limited.

When I trade my time for money, I have the money but I no longer have the time.

Let's say I want to buy a car and I trade money for the car. Now I've traded it for a depreciating liability. This is why poor people stay that way.

There is a better way. If you want to create wealth, here's how you do it.

When I want money, I don't take time, but instead I'll create an idea. If I can create something and I solve their problem, they will pay me some of their money. I find a big pool of people with a big problem and solve that problem. I obsess over that problem. While they are sleeping or eating I solve that problem then I show it to them.

People who have deep pockets are willing to pay some of that money to solve their problem.

When I create this solution, let's say I write a book. Now I've created a reproducible asset, then I sell the book and people give me money.

My wealth is multiplying because I am a resource.

I learned this formula from Daniel Priestly - Income Follows Assets

Where do assets come from?

Mindset + Skillset + Toolset = Assets

I have creativity in unlimited supply, and I have a large number of books. The more I use my creativity to create assets, the more money I produce.

How many of you were making money 19 years ago? How many, with that work, still make money today?

I wrote this book, "From The Trashman To The Cashman". I sold insurance and investments at night and learned the magic of compound interest. I wrote this book in 2006, 19 years ago. This book makes me $110K a year. I did the work once and I still get paid for it every day.

How many of you worked and still get paid for the work you did in 2021? I wrote a book in 2021 called BOSS Moves. It's 172 pages and sells for $30. This book funnel makes me $500K a year for work I did 4 years ago.

This is what I do and these are just some of the assets I have. You have to look for my offers. I'm a ninja offer maker. The more offers I create, the more wealth I create. Money is not wealth. Wealth is your ability to create value for someone other than yourself.

I hate cliches. They sound good the first time, but terrible afterwards. "You just need to create more value". But what's valuable to the people you are making the offer to? In order to know that, I have to know where value comes from.

Why do some people value reading and others don't? Why do some people love cars and others don't? I hate flying commercial so I only fly private. I know it's expensive but I don't care. Why do I value flying private so much that I'd rather pay $110K flying round trip to Vegas?

Values come from past perceived voids creating present perceived values. If I feel like something was missing in the past, I will value it more now.

That's why having conversations with your customers is so valuable. You are talking about something they care about instead of getting them to care about something you talk about.

My dream car is a 1968 Pontiac GTO. I've wanted this car since I was 17 years old. I'm 63 now and this has been a long time. I finally found it for $40,000 and I bought it because I wanted it as a kid and I couldn't have it. Then I get in it, and the suspension is all loosey goosey but I don't care, because this is my dream.

Present perceived virtues create present perceived values. Things that I think are good right now. For me, I don't like people wasting my time. I'm 63, so I'm closer to 100 than 10 years old. So going to the airport and wasting hours waiting on a plane that might get canceled doesn't make sense to me.

My clients pay me $40K an hour. If I go to the airport and get there 2 hours early, I've wasted $80K. So what happened is I just flushed away $160K to save $110K. I don't love spending that but I'd rather do that than sit at the airport and get accosted by a TSA agent who wishes they were a CIA agent.

Future perceived visions create present perceived values. You can see something great happening in the future.

To fill the voids of our past, to find the visions of our future, we are willing to pay for that.

Poor people and middle class people feel like everything is expensive because they pay for things with money they have exchanged their time for. That means when I look at a car, if I make $100K a year and that car costs the same, I'm asking myself "is this car worth 1 year of my life?" If I look at a house and it's a $500K house, is this worth 5 years of my life? My subconscious is asking the question.

The reason you feel like that is you feel pain for every hour you spend away from your family to pay for that thing. I'd recommend you tap into your creativity because you have an infinite supply.

To wealthy creative entrepreneurs everything costs the same amount.

Because I pay for things according to my creativity, which means I still have the creativity after I create the thing. I create the offer, I get the money, and I pay for things according to my creativity so it doesn't matter if I'm buying a pack of tic tacs or a private plane fare - it doesn't matter how much it costs.

What if your perspective was "everything costs the same amount?" It costs according to my creativity and I have an unlimited supply. I write a book or create a coaching course and it pays for whatever.

We were going on vacation and instead of going for 10 days, we went for 14 days. I said "Why don't we do a 2 day event for $25K?" 10 people bought the offer and we got paid because we were going on vacation anyway.

That's what I call a paid vacation.

The reason I hate flying is because I flew to Dallas to speak at a real estate seminar and it was a nonstop flight with one checked bag. I got to Dallas and my luggage wasn't there. They called me 2 months later and still didn't have it. It had my favorite suit in it, too.

A month after that, the bag came back. It has mold on my suit and it was stupid. I'd paid for this level of service.

Then I had an event in Cincinnati and my son rented a yacht for my birthday. Our first flight got delayed and now I'm going to miss getting on the yacht with my son. That's when I said I'll never do this again. I had an event coming up in Vegas. Two weeks before that I called my friend Gary who had access to a jet. He said it would be $60K, then he said "You got to put your big boy pants on if you're going to fly private".

So, now I have a decision to make. I created an offer and the offer is called VIP Day+. This was in June 2022, and I said it's only $200,000. Two people bought it.

Because I was speaking at someone else's event I had them pay for half the flight. So I made $370K to fly private.

Then 16 people bought that offer. And I started charging the people who wanted me to fly to them, $11K an hour. I've done over $12M in offers. I raised the price to $350K in 2023 and this year to $375K.

My offer philosophy - if the people you sell your offer to, can't 10X their return, then the price is too high. Last year on our $350K VIP day, we sold 20 of them.

I'm thinking how can I provide so much value to these people that it's a no brainer for them to pay me?

If you will master these 4 offers, being broke will be virtually an impossibility for the rest of your life.

If your business is not doing well:

1. You don't have enough people to talk to
2. You have an offer but you don't have a good one
3. You're not good at telling people the transformation
4. You sell a lot but you don't make enough money

Offer 1 - Lead Generation Offer (LGO)

This is the thing you sell in exchange for their attention. TIP - stop using the word "Free" in your marketing. Even with YouTube offers, you have to pay with your attention. Let's say I'm going to do a presentation, it makes more sense to sell a ticket to a webinar, event etc. But you are scared to charge for your webinar. We have 300 a month that buy our challenge tickets, then show up.

Lead Magnet - in order to get it, they give you your name, email and phone number. Only the serious need apply.

The #1 problem with lead generation is because your potential prospects, all of your LGOs are leading towards pleasure. For example: "7 steps to 7 figures".

If someone doesn't know who you are, people are going to think it's a scam. They don't know you, like you or trust you.

Most of your LGOs should be for cold traffic, and lead them from pain.

Work with human nature and human nature will work for you.

Example: The 7 Biggest Mistakes Entrepreneurs Are Making That Keep Them From Making 7 Figures

This will convert much better than "The 7 Steps To 7 Figures"

Offer #2 - Core Product Offer (CPO)

This is the main thing you sell that makes you money.

- If I want to make a $1M, I have to sell 50K of my $20 offer.
- If I sell 5,000 of a $200, I make the same but the work is less.
- If I sell a $2,000 home study course, I only to sell 500 of them to make $1M.

- What if I turn it into a $20,000 mastermind.
- Or a $200,000 VIP day?

I do all of it. This is how you make money with a core product.

Offer #3 - Premium Value Offer (PVO)

We only sold one $1M offer last year. Stop talking about high ticket offers. Who gets the benefit of this? You do.

With a premium value offer, the client gets the value. So it makes more sense to call it what it actually is. If you are good at selling but you are unable to deliver, that's not a good offer. But if you can deliver, why would you want those people to go somewhere else?

People wrestle with this in their brain. The first time I did this, I offered it for $3,000 and 2 people bought it. The next time I ran the event I offered it for $4,000 and 7 people bought it.

Most entrepreneurs don't understand the value of their offer. They show the process or name everything in the offer. Your offer only has one real source of value and that's the payoff. Start talking about what they get.

When you observe the facts, it's in the frame of a focus in your head. There's no such thing as a bad or good fact. It's impossible for anything to exist with one side.

You manufacture a belief if you are focused on either positive or negative. Positive is faith and negative is doubt.

They are both beliefs. Faith is belief in the outcome you desire, doubt is belief in the outcome you don't desire.

The feeling in your heart is the thing that raises everything. Humans are singularly motivated. People do things for one reason - because they feel like it. At the end of the day, you're going to do the thing you feel like doing.

Faith will translate into your heart as a feeling of anticipation. When you are writing that book and see people buying it you don't get writer's block.

If you are focused on negative aspects it's producing a feeling in your heart called anxiety. Fear is caution over a real and present danger. Anxiety is caution over future imagined danger.

The focus is my head creates the feeling in my heart and that creates a function in my hands. When I'm focused on positive, the function is power. When it's negative, anxiety creates powerlessness.

I got this from Romans Chapter VI.

I used this as you, but now this person is your client. You are off to the side and everything you say is causing them to either have anticipation to buy your offer or anxiety to not buy your offer, and that's the power of making offers.

Russell Brunson & Todd Dickerson

Imagine being in the room ten years ago? We've created something amazing that's going to change your lives. As the head of ClickFunnels, my job is to convince you guys that you can actually do this. I'm the belief cheerleader.

When you see all the Two Comma Club award winners get on stage, it'll change your belief system. When we first created the award we had 79 winners.

About 17 years ago, we were trying to build this idea, but it never happened because technology wasn't ready for it. About a year and half ago, one night we were talking about the future. We brought up this thing we were all trying to do and started brainstorming. About a year ago, they figured it out.

I'm really bad at keeping secrets and what we are about to share is already done. We wanted to tell you at Funnel Hacking Live International but decided to wait. To put this thing together I wanted the person who designed it for you guys to help me, Kevin Richards.

You are hearing about it about a month before anyone else will hear about it.

Kevin Richards

If you have an offer that you are selling online, raise your hand. Now raise it again, if someone else now is promoting your offer for you. There's way less people. How many would like others to promote your offer?

Back in the day, we all started building this business and internet marketing was originally JV with affiliate promotions. We all became friends and helped build each other's businesses along the way. ClickFunnels for the first several years was built with zero advertising. It was affiliates sending traffic to Russell doing daily webinars.

Then everything changed. About 5-6 years ago, we all felt it. We started to think we could get the same traffic that our affiliates were sending to us. We could just run ads on Facebook or Google instead of giving 50% to affiliates. So we lost the power of recommendations and went transactional.

I saw we had the opportunity to change all that, by bringing back affiliate marketing and creating something entirely new.

Grant Cardone held his big challenge. We put our free offer and put it on the challenge page of his challenge funnel. People registered for his challenge, they would get a free CF account and that was it. He became the #1 affiliate for the next year.

We moved a few years ago, and my wife wanted to make new friends. So she played pickleball and loved it. She started a brand and was selling shirts. Her average cart value was an issue. So while she was trying to make her funnel work, she was making friends along the way.

She met Sarah who was making custom pickleball paddles. They tried to promote for each other but couldn't get it to work. They met Sam who had a course to become a better player, but also couldn't get his funnel to work.

Then they met Paul, who rents really nice homes that have access to pickleball courts and holds retreats to become better at it. Once Molly was able to figure out if she could promote the other people the right way, she could change the way she ran her business.

So they created a collaboration. If Molly could offer the paddle, course and event in one big funnel, she goes from a $6 profit to $67 profit. The paddle is a 50/50 split, and it's the same with the course.

When I saw that opportunity combined with what we are trying to do with the technology, we figured out a name for it called OfferLab.

Russell Brunson

Imagine if you can take everyone's products and put it into one funnel. There's 4 steps

1. Add your offer
2. Go to co-lab library and pick different offers
3. Create an offer stack/funnel
4. Promote

Imagine if you have a place where everyone's offers are there. In 30 seconds you can build an offer stack and when sales come through, the money is split along the line.

Inside OfferLab

We give you templates and all you do is fill in the information. It's much easier to use. Every funnel has been taking 20 minutes to build. You have the best technology partnering with Stripe.

You can manage your entire affiliate payout process on OfferLab and we do it for you. There's no CSV files, no math, no PayPal payouts. We pay the affiliate when it's time to pay them out. There's no fallout with tracking issues. Every affiliate gets their own unique funnel so they can use their own ad tracking, domains. There's full integration into every platform and you get full sales reporting from it.

Click the Offers button and you start telling us about your offer. Put the name in and integrate with your current platform. We integrate with GHL, Shopify and ClickFunnels as well. Everything on the platform happens automatically.

If you don't have integrations you can add them individually. You don't have to have any of those platforms to sell, you can just start with an idea. Start with basic products and descriptions. Just that first step gives you the ability to have a full offer with a full checkout.

Step 2 - CoLab - look for things to promote. It's like a marketplace where you are finding other people's offers. You are looking for things in your market. We called this collaborative commerce where you are working with people who were previously your competition. Find offers that will work together with you. When you request to promote it, it gets added to your offer library.

Step 3 - Create the offer stack - In 30 seconds, the entire funnel is done. How many of your customers love you to death, but they know nothing about marketing? There's a ton of use cases for this. You don't have to do anything else, just drag and drop the icons OTO or order bump. You don't have to write copy, as they've already done that step.

Step 4 - Promote - grab your link and start promoting. There can be 3 different creators with 3 different things to sell, and once the buyer buys, everyone gets paid automatically.

One of the biggest questions we get is when someone buys, what about the thank you page? There's a different block on the thank you page that shows each thing they bought. This is literally one of the fastest ways that I've seen to make money.

The opportunity to do this is to show the people you are promoting that they can make more money by promoting their offers. It's not just about you making more money. You can leverage this platform and go to your inmarket competitors and make them JV partners through the platform.

What if it was free?

Our official launch is 30 days away.
We want to make sure our offer is on the platform before launch day.
We make our money from processing fees, so the more you sell, the more we make.

- Processing fee is 3% + $.30
- Your affiliate pays 1% on payout
- $4.95 fee when you pull money out
- We charge you $0 and Stripe pays that
- And you get an OfferLab debit card

Trent Shelton
Self Worth Mastery

I don't care what level you are at, there's a you inside of you that you haven't met yet and that's the greatest you.

Mastering your self worth isn't about changing who you are. It's about realizing the power that's always been inside you and finally stepping into it.

You are enough. When you leave here, you need to make sure this is not just some inspiration. Application creates transformation. If you don't, your life will stay the same.

When I talk about self worth mastery, it's the thing that changed my life. My inbox is full of people that don't know their worth. A lot of people tie it to how much money they have or how many followers, but no matter how much it won't fill their soul.

A lot of us have relationships, grief, burnout, or stress that is controlling how we feel about ourselves.

Never let how people feel about you, friends, strangers…change how you feel about yourself.

Intrinsic Value (IV) - I believe this is the greatest contributor to your success. I'm talking about living in fulfillment. When you walk inside your house, you should love your environment. There's no point in having 12 million followers if my kids don't like me. If the people around me that mean the most to me don't like me, there's no point.

If you talked to me ten years ago, my self worth was low. I would have heard what Russell said but I didn't feel it was possible for me.

You will rise to the level of your aspirations and dreams, and you will always fall down to the level that you set for yourself. When you leave here, if your self worth is low, you'll never believe what someone else tells you.

1. SB - Self Belief - most people's self belief level is at a 3. That's when people bring you something that seems impossible and you disconnect because you don't believe it's real for you.

2. ST - Self Trust - you don't trust yourself. How do you deal with social anxiety? I trust myself and I know God will bring me through it. So I trust the plan for myself even when the plan doesn't make sense. I know some of you struggle and you've come here for an answer. You have so much doubt, anxiety, adversity and a lot of us believe our circumstances. Mine told me I could never be a motivational speaker.

3. SC - Self Confidence - your confidence level is too low. I believe there's a magnet inside you that people can see. How many of you have confidence even in your biggest fears? How many of you have confidence when your backs are against the wall? Even when adversity shows up, I realize it's just another opportunity. Most people operate at 30% when it comes to their self worth. If you get a chance, make sure you take that self assessment test.

5 Rules To Living Legendary

In 2009, I was a football player but I got cut. I didn't know what to do with my life. I looked in the mirror and said "It all starts with you."

Rule 1 - take massive ownership over your life. We live in a world where everyone wants to point the finger. It's everyone's fault. But it's all your fault. It takes your power back. A lot of us live like this, where it's everyone else's fault.

I was blaming the coaches and everyone else, but when I pointed the fault to myself, it changed me. I know it's hard to accept this. If you are the problem, you are also the solution. If you are blaming your ex or your job, no one cares anymore about your sad story.

People kept living, time kept ticking, the world kept spinning and the bills kept coming. So I took the power back from those things and took ownership over my life.

Boundaries aren't walls to keep things out, they are bridges to let the right things in.

A lot of us live where we are setting boundaries to protect your soul. Some of you are too accessible. The email can wait if you really trust yourself. So can the text message. It can wait. Some of us are slaves to requests. We are professional people pleasers. And you wonder why you don't have energy for the things that matter.

Before 12 PM you can't reach me unless you are family or in an emergency. I know I have energy for my family. 77% of people are burnt out by 12 PM. At 12PM, I'm just getting started.

The second thing I'm going to talk about, is this is a picture of my best friend who committed suicide. In a world of so much fun, people need the real you. Some of you think you inspire, but you inspire from your struggle. You are meant to be a human, not a robot.

If you allow adversity to stop you, your mission isn't strong enough. Every time there is an opportunity to stand against the wall, you crumble. I made a commitment to my boy, and said I'm going to live the rest of my life doing this.

I don't care what the stage is, just because you lose something doesn't mean you have to lose your life. I know we have people struggling with this. You are one choice away from a new beginning. And you are a commitment away from a new life.

Keep giving tomorrow another chance until it changes your life. The reason why I stay loyal is because I made a commitment, not just a promise. There is no other choice. That was my commitment to him

The 3 C's - Every person I see that is living a legendary life, has these:

1. Care - They care about people. You can tell how much by the way they treat their clients and employees. I know Russell and Todd and the way they show up for people. They care for this mission.

2. Commitment - this is staying loyal to what you said you were going to do, long after you started. If your reason is just to make money, it's not strong enough.

3. Conviction - I grew up with Bruce Lee. Back in 1984, if you were watching this movie, he gets the glow at the end. He's tapping into the highest level of himself. Everyone's glow is different but it's conviction in their soul. Have you met someone that just seems different and you are magnetized by them?

I'm not the most talented speaker, but I'm on a lot of stages because I have conviction in my soul. If you have conviction, you will make the world respect you.

That's a picture of me with glasses, and those are my wife's glasses. I'm wearing her glasses and what's wild is my wife is visually challenged. So I put on her glasses, which she had just bought and I couldn't see anything. She told me something that changed my life. She said you aren't supposed to see, they are not your prescription. I see perfectly fine with them.

I believe that God gave you a vision. Don't worry about the how, just trust the who. I believe that a lot of you here have that vision. The mistake a lot of us make is we take all of our spiritual prescription that's been given to us, and we take off our lenses and give it some proximity. We go to the people closest to us to validate what we see.

What happens is, they are not qualified.

Stop bringing your vision to people who are not visionaries. Stop bringing your dreams to people who are not dreamers.

My NFL dream was put down by so many teachers. I made that happen because I didn't allow a teacher who had never played to put it down. When I said I wanted to be a speaker, I was told I had to change the way I talked, put on a suit, and go to ToastMasters, but that's not me. It's very hard trying to be something you are not. No one can beat you at being you.

I believe I have greatness inside me. God gave me a vision and I expect I can do it.

Instead of us putting our glasses back on, we keep them in our pocket the rest of our lives, unsure, unclear and lost. Because you allowed someone to take a prescription from you that wasn't theirs to take.

Some of you are hearing these things where your neurological connection is going back to your past. I'm not good enough. Who am I?

Then, there's professional people pleasers. People are not going to like you, but who cares. Our brain is so focused on what's going wrong that we can't focus on what's going right. The one person who says something bad on your post is not your client.

The last set of lenses is your power lenses. No matter what I go through I'm going to keep showing up. Put your glasses back on. Don't let anyone be the narrator of your life. I don't care if you've had some bad chapters. Just because you've had some bad chapters, doesn't mean your story can't end well.

You don't have a consistency problem. You showed up at something you hate everyday. Or some of us continued with relationships that sucked.

Consistency is your greatest super power. If you can be consistent with the things you hate - a bad job, etc. - why can't you be consistent with the things that will improve you?

1. It doesn't mean that much to you, or
2. You don't understand what it's costing you not to show up

If it isn't a hell yeah, then it's a hell no. I don't do average. Coming here was a hell yeah for me.

I talked about adversity, and if you are going to be legendary, you need to embrace it. If you don't have adversity, you are playing small. In 2021, my mother inspired my book but she wasn't alive to see that book be printed. So I'm reading her that book to her at her final resting place.

Another time, my daughter was in the ICU. Right after I got the call that my mother had passed, I got a call that Maya had passed out. As I'm running over there, I see a small figure not moving. My 4 year old daughter was bleeding and unconscious. I remember getting down and picking her up.

I kept asking God why and I realized, stop asking God why me. Start asking God, Why not me? My daughter had been playing in the backyard, and when my neighbor mowed his lawn he went over a big rock that flew up and hit her in the head. When I picked her up, she gave me a kiss like it was normal. She went to the ICU for 5 days.

During that time, my grandmother passed away. Appreciate the storms because they also produce growth. The good news was that Maya was healed from the rock but the bad news was that Maya has a tumor. The rock was a gift which brought us there. We discovered the tumor because of the rock. Now she is tumor free, because we caught it early.

There's some things in your life, but my gifts are always great. You have a gift of legendary that's wrapped in adversity. Go live your best life and make the world respect your greatness. It all starts with you.

Russell Brunson
One to Many Selling

In today's session, we are going to fill out the papers that are scanned inside these notes. We are going to be talking about the One to Many Selling Online presentation.

If you don't know how to sell the offer, it's kind of useless. The first thing to understand is the offer you are selling, when you understand what it is, it makes it easier. You have to think about your hero's journey. You went on a journey and figured out your thing.

You started going down the path, came to a dead end and you kept trying it over and over. A few years ago, when Kaelin Poulin launched Lady Boss, she said that women tried to lose weight 8 times a year. It's the same with people starting a business. You as the hero are trying to figure out how to get the thing, and over time you figure out how to to get the result and you achieve the thing.

The most valuable thing happened to you during this journey. This is what I like to call - a map. The by-product of getting there is the map. Whenever you are selling any offer, what you are selling is the map.

After you have this map and you are talking to your dream customer in the future, these are just people. They typically have tried 10 different things and they haven't worked. So you have this map and the way you make this map exciting, you have to convince them that your map is the way.

I did the Linchpin presentation, and said this is the way. The map you have is better than anyone's else. The only thing that works is my map. I'm not trying to convince them of a thousand things, I'm only trying to convince them that my map is the best way.

Hook, Story, Offer

This is the most simple framework and if we reverse engineer it, we have our offer and we need to tell the story. But you first need the hook. Think about when people are scrolling, you need to grab their attention, something to get them to stop their scroll just long enough to tell them the story.

I remember telling people when others would hire me, they would say their offer wasn't working. If the funnel isn't working, one of the steps is broken, it's either the hook, story or offer. Then we look at those things and retweak it. Eventually it converts and then you grow.

The Perfect Webinar Framework

Since we introduced this, people have made crazy money in almost any industry.

The first thing we do is tell the origin story about how we discovered the map. Second, we tell the story of how the map works.

If you look at it, there's hook and story over and over, then the offer at the end.

Yesterday, McCall Jones talked about the book, If You Give A Mouse A Cookie. The premise of all these books are the same thing.

The first component of your offer is the cookie - the thing they want the most. The map might be a course, and everytime you give something it solves a solution and introduces a problem they didn't know they had.

I gave you this map and now you know how to get there, but you need hiking boots, Next you need a canteen of water, then what else? Maybe a compass.

When I sell my books, I create an offer stack and here's all the things they need along the journey. It's the same thing with my webinars.

If I'm doing a 90 minute webinar, 30 minutes will be spent presenting the stack.

An offer without a story is useless. The story increases the perceived value of what you are going to sell. To get someone to run to the back for a table rush, this is what you need:

1. Origin story - It's about how you discovered the map. What did you have to go through? Your dream customer is you, five years ago. This is the first 15 minutes of the presentation.

2. Now we teach the map. We have the map story and the steps. When I teach funnel hacks, I tell the story about Funnel Hacking and the first step is finding a funnel that works, then the second step, etc. That will be the next 15 minutes of your presentation. Sometimes the story is about myself, sometimes it's about one

of my successful students. The next thing is now we have to tell the story of how they can do it.

3. Why do they think this won't work for them? Now, I have to show them I'm not technical either. I tell that story and show them the step by step process and a demo of how it works. You are showing them the process to break that internal false belief.

4. Next you have to talk about their external false beliefs, then tell them a story where at the end, they can do it. What story do you have that trumps their false beliefs? You don't need to get the slides perfect, if you just know these 4 pieces, you can crush it.

Hooks

Every story you tell, needs a hook to get people to actually listen to it. What are the hooks you have? Every good story has 2-3 dozen hooks.

Example: My Weird Niche Funnel That Made $X

Different hook, same story. We need to figure out what's the hook for each story. When I'm creating a presentation, I have the hook slide, my 3 secrets then the offer slide. These are the most important ones.

We need a hook for your origin story, then the hooks for your following stories.

You have the foundation to create a one to many presentation:

- Offer
- Origin
- 3 stories
- Hooks

Eileen Wilder

How many of you, when you speak on video, podcast or stages, want the crowd to go crazy and buy your stuff? I'm going to show you how to make your speaking highly addictive using storytelling. If you don't do this, you will be boring.

This storytelling framework helped me go from being a broke mother of 3 to selling millions of dollars. You will never be broke again if you put this presentation into place. When I came to FHL in 2018, I was broke and my husband was Uber driving. I sat in the back and didn't understand a thing.

I heard someone say 'ideal customer avatar' and 'joint venture partnerships', but they were also talking about coaching. I thought maybe there were a lot of sports involved. So if you are new, I got you.

I heard them ask "What ails you?" and I had nothing to do with being sick or wrong. What ails you is that you are living your lives as amateurs.

My biggest problem was that I was hiding. When you are hiding, you rob the world of your calling, creativity and contribution. When you hide, you don't even know what your voice sounds like.

Turn pro in your own mind. You have to call yourself a pro before anyone else will. You're a pro when you say that - Steven Pressfield talks about this in his book.

So I made a janky video. Do you ever look at your stuff then look at the guru stuff online? They look so perfect and they sound so smart and articulate. No one was thinking those thoughts looking at my video. I was so terrible, and people told me about it.

So I studied how pros and amateurs did it and I learned why amateurs were doing wrong:

Amateurs - the #1 killer of sales is over teaching - telling information without transformation

Pro - have stories that made the audience feel pain, excitement, hope and like buying

The limbic system is most active when making a buying decision and will override the logical part of the brain. This means if you can tell stories that make them feel like they will buy, they will do so.

The pros have a pattern and I noticed they did the same thing.

BITS - Belief and Identity Transformation System

I figured this out and people bought, then I got invited onto podcasts and big stages. I remember this one event and I was watching this storytelling framework set people free. When the host came on the stage with the offer, hundreds and hundreds ran to buy. I finally felt like a pro.

This is learnable and trainable and you can learn it now.

Speaking is the skill that pays the bills. If you can speak like this, they will feel like buying.

My bank account went crazy along with the crowds. You have to allow yourself to stop hiding and go pro. The only thought I want you to have now is that "I can do it, because I'm about to be rich."

When I shared this framework, Russell said it was the most profound framework he's seen.

Part 1 - most people when they start telling their story, talk about being broke and struggling but use the word "I" a lot. Or a lot of people say the word "Me" a lot. Great speakers shift from "I" to "You".

Go from "I was broke and struggling" to "Have you ever been in a place where you were struggling and you felt trapped, and stressed out?" Almost no one does this. Have you ever been talking to someone and thought "I wonder when this person will be done?"

It's because they haven't shifted to "You" fast enough. When you shift to the word "You" the audience goes internal. The audience sees the landscape of their life because you are expressing the story using the word "You".

Next, the whole part of the story is to tell their story. Before you get to the point, bounce back.

For example, "I went to FHL. Have you ever been to an event where the speakers were so mesmerizing? There was this guy Russell and I didn't know what was happening but I'm going all in".

The point of your story is what you want the audience to believe. Most speakers will state their point and tell the audience what to do. Most speakers will say "You need a funnel". Audiences say "I'm 100% not doing it" so you want to weave the point into the story.

"I heard Russell talking about funnels being confusing, but you can weave in stories and it will convert!" Now they are hearing funnels are awesome.

The Soundbite - your audience will get so excited when you do this. This is the enemy the tribe can unite against. Then you want to have a soundbite. I used rhymezone.com for this.

Soundbite Stack

- Famous quote
- Famous quote
- Your quote

Example:

- W. Clement Stone said: "Do it now"
- Napoleon Hill said: "Whatever the mind of man can conceive and believe, it can achieve"
- I like to say: "Procrastination is the assassination of your destination."

1. I
2. You
3. Point
4. Tribe
5. Soundbite

Master Key

One time a client asked me "What if I mess it up?" I said I can teach you the master key to sales. Sales is the transference of energy.

Communication is only 7% verbal and 93% non verbal. We can get our words wrong but if we get our energy right, we win.

Command Energy: It's not a needy energy, it's a leader energy.

Once upon a time there was a guy named Gideon. He was hiding but an angel showed up and told him he was a warrior. The point is you don't even know who you are. Gideon says "But I am the least in my house."

Whatever follows the words "I am", is determining the direction of your direction.

Some of you might be hiding behind excuses. I'm not qualified, I'm not smart, I don't show up…etc.

So the angel has a cure. He says "Get up!" In Hebrew this means shake yourself from the dust. I want you all to shake off the past. You are a powerhouse and you need to stop hiding, with your addiction to affliction.

Get up!
Go now. In the strength that you have
Go save your people
Get louder than your enemies

You need to get some spirit and say come at me. I refuse to tolerate the tyranny of average amateurs. Mediocre men will not determine my destiny.

You weren't born for the shadows.
You were born for the stage.
You weren't born for the silence.
You were born for the battle.
You weren't born to hesitate.
You were born to dominate.

Decide to go pro right now.

Shake off what people think about you and decide to go pro now.

Armand Morin
The Stack

I've been speaking online for years and have done about $100M from speaking. To make more than some people that make in ten years is crazy and there was one thing I discovered, called The Stack.

I'm going to show you a presentation that has done over $3M in sales. You cannot show the stack without showing products.

What is the Stack? It's a value builder and a way to create shock and value.

The Pieces Of The Stack

- The Product
- The Bonuses
- The Price Value
- The Drop
- The Final Price

The Product

Let's assume you have a great product. You have to stretch your product. You have to get the most mileage out of this product.

I have a product. It's called Tube Entrepreneur. You can't buy this, I'm using it for a presentation.

Who Is This Program For?

- If…You want to use this system to generate massive traffic to any website, product or service
- If…You are an author…INCREASE BOOK SALES
- If..You are a coach….INCREASE CLIENTS
- If…You are a speaker….BE #1 IN YOUR NICHE

Sell this to local businesses and create an incredible monthly income in the process.

Here's my close:

I tell them about the product, and give them lifetime access. You need to do this. How much does it cost you? Nothing. People will buy just for that reason alone. It sounds amazing!

Then I tell them they will get the other products. I'm stretching each detail and it seems much bigger than it actually is.

If you join me today, you'll get…X, Y & Z.

Then I say "What if.." It forces people to pay attention.

I talk about being Filipino and I'm going to show you how to outsource.

I'm summarizing the entire system to show them what they are getting.

Instant Access To My System

- Complete Online Video Training
- My secret YouTube ranking system
- The formula needed to rank any term literally in seconds after uploading
- Ranking factors
- How to rank tough keyword phrases
- Creating direct response videos

How much value do they feel now after I broke it down individually?

Then they will also receive LIFETIME access. It's free lifetime customer support. How much does it cost for this? It doesn't cost you anything but it makes the customer want to buy because they feel secure.

I show them what they will learn with my system:

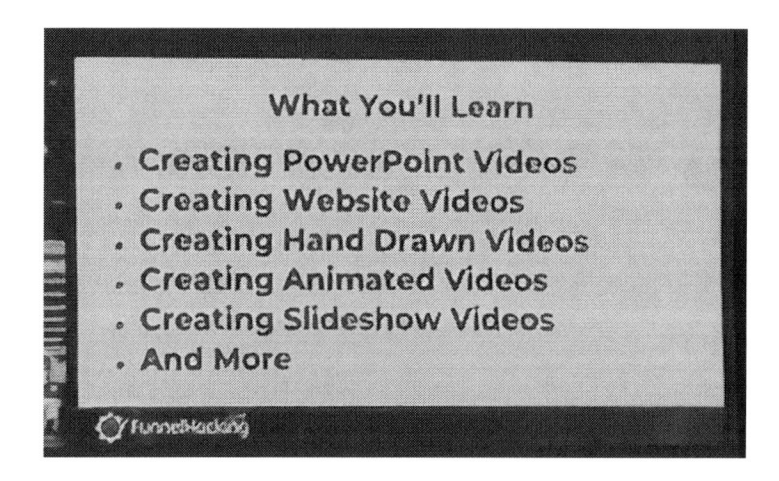

> **What You'll Learn**
> - Creating PowerPoint Videos
> - Creating Website Videos
> - Creating Hand Drawn Videos
> - Creating Animated Videos
> - Creating Slideshow Videos
> - And More

TIP: If you start, "Hi, my name is X", this will increase your sales by 67% at the start of each webinar.

I go onto the next part. Start using the word "Exclusive". It stops people from shopping. If they watch your webinar, they are already thinking of shopping. Now they can't get this anywhere else except from you.

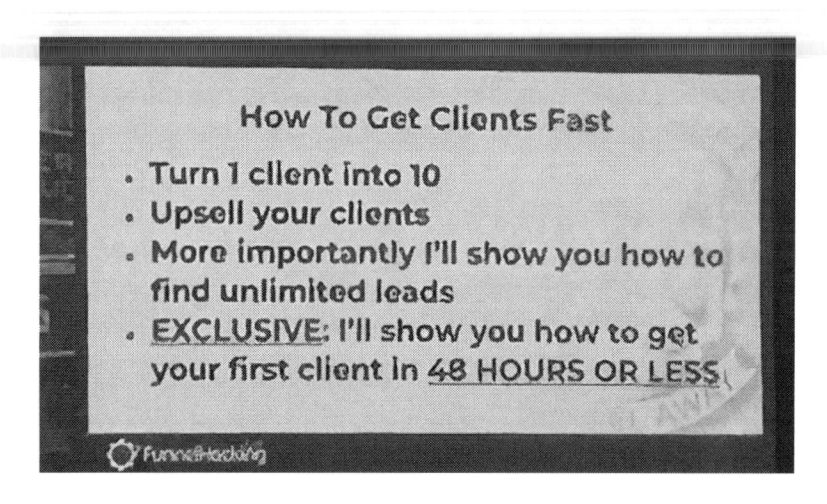

> **How To Get Clients Fast**
> - Turn 1 client into 10
> - Upsell your clients
> - More importantly I'll show you how to find unlimited leads
> - EXCLUSIVE: I'll show you how to get your first client in 48 HOURS OR LESS

I take my membership and break it down to make it feel like more. The size of your stack matters! Also, you need real world pricing. If you haven't sold it before, don't inflate prices.

Add: Exclusive Bonus: Today only!

If a person leaves and doesn't buy, they are probably not going to buy.

Say: "For the first few people who join me today…"

Every word you use has to earn its place. John Carlton told me this. There are no words in this presentation that are unnecessary. You have to be careful what you say because some will make the mistake of saying "For the next 12 people…" but what if 13 people buy?

So when I say the "First few people" it's implied urgency.

Next they get access to our seminar. If you are doing a seminar, how much does it cost? Nothing. But what does it do for you? They sell to the audience. Then I say PLUS one more thing…

Steve Jobs always did this with his presentations with Apple. But wait! There's one more thing!

If You Join Me Today...

- Give you all ads to hire sales people for FREE
- How to hire appointment setters for FREE
- How to setup your AGENCY
- Get up and running in days
- I'll show the work flow to handle every step of the process nothing is left unturned
- Leverage your business in Millions

You want to get to where people think you are finished and then stop and keep going. You want them to assume the offer is too good and you are crazy. I want people to gasp when they are at a live audience.

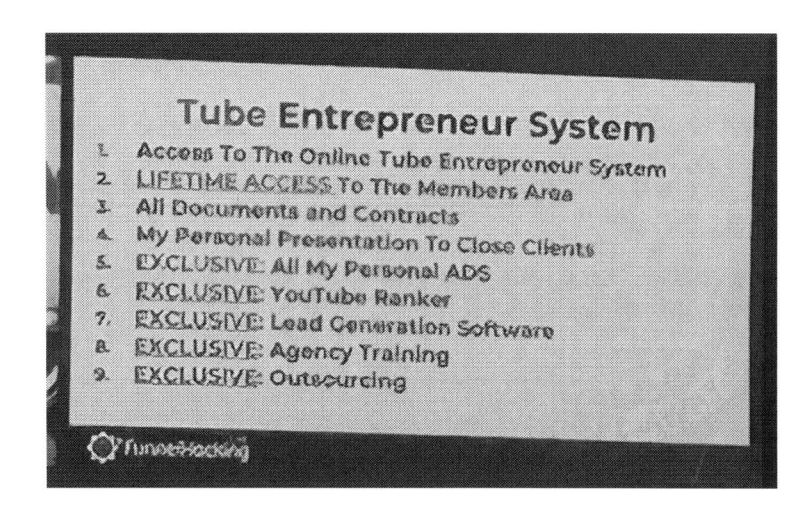

Tube Entrepreneur System

1. Access To The Online Tube Entrepreneur System
2. LIFETIME ACCESS To The Members Area
3. All Documents and Contracts
4. My Personal Presentation To Close Clients
5. EXCLUSIVE: All My Personal ADS
6. EXCLUSIVE: YouTube Ranker
7. EXCLUSIVE: Lead Generation Software
8. EXCLUSIVE: Agency Training
9. EXCLUSIVE: Outsourcing

Then I tell them about the marketing cruise they can attend. Then we review what you'll receive today. The stack is not just a stack of things. When I first started speaking, the close was very short and it was a 5-10 minute close. Eventually it went to 30 minutes just closing.

The problem is when you have people in an audience, they forget what they were actually buying. So I had this idea, why don't we itemize this? I created this piece, listing everything on an invoice so you could see the value.

Each time you do the stack, you do it faster. Why? Because it gets more exciting. It's like classical music. It starts slow and builds up at the end. It's the same with your close.

Total Everything Up on your stack.

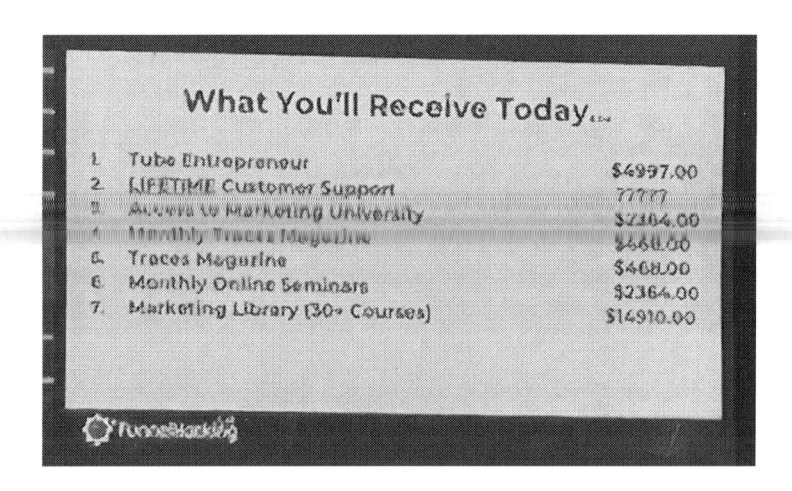

What You'll Receive Today...

1.	Tube Entrepreneur	$4997.00
2.	LIFETIME Customer Support	?????
3.	Access to Marketing University	$2364.00
4.	Monthly Traces Magazine	$468.00
5.	Traces Magazine	$468.00
6.	Monthly Online Seminars	$2364.00
7.	Marketing Library (30+ Courses)	$14910.00

Is it better to be first or last? It gets people thinking and talking in their head.

You'll get everything today for:

Total value: $30,961
Today only: $4,997

We are setting it up for a drop.

> **Total Everything Up...**
>
> - It Would Cost Upwards of $30,000+
> - I charge $10,000 a day with huge numbers of people paying me that every single year
> - I'm looking for only a FEW PEOPLE right now to become to be the FIRST to start in the UK
>
> **Is It Better To Be First or Last?**

I say I'm going to do something special for today only. For the first few people who get up, buy, etc. because I'm here…I want to do something special.

This is the drop and this is the easiest way to do this.

I say, because you are here with Russell, I want to do something special. Instead of paying what everyone else pays, once you make your first $10,000, you must agree to send me your testimonial. Now they are wondering what is this special offer? So they agree to send me a testimonial and now it's only $1,997.

Every time you offer a big price, people don't buy. I want mine to be the lowest price. So I will help you finance it. I don't say 3 payments of $797. I say to just put down $797 today. And then it's two more payments of $797. Now I went from $1,997 all the way down to $797 and it makes it sound better.

One final time I go through everything they get, you'll be one of the first people to use the system and you have two choices. You can pay $1,997 today or $797 and two more payments of $797.

Ashley Kirkwood

I have identified an enemy to greatness and it's called sameness. This is where you do everything in your power to fit in. In school and at work, have you ever felt like you had to conform? Have you ever felt like you needed to speak quietly? Have you ever felt like who you were wasn't enough?

The thing about being an entrepreneur is that we are part of the 1% crazy. I looked up the word crazy and I found that word comes from the root word craze - which means to break. Over time you would break your mind. But in recent times, we popularized the word by saying that guy is crazy and that's a good thing.

As entrepreneurs we have to break the mold. When I watched the video for this event, Russell said we are the radical ones. It's okay to go a little crazy sometimes and stand out.

If you are ready to stand out, let me hear you scream. All of you screamed but none of you stood up. How many of you want to help your clients change their life? How many want your clients to not work with someone you don't trust?

I want Katherine to just join me up on stage and I want you to imagine that Katherine represents customers you love, and that she has a problem. In your mind you want her to stop, but she keeps ignoring you. She's ignoring you because maybe you can't stand out.

There are some of you that need to be bolder and louder. I want to take Katherine and get loud, really gaudy and annoying and I want you to get on my bus. She gets on my bus and because it's so large, we're going to get more friends on the bus.

Now we're all on the bus. But it came from L.A. and it was inconvenient. How many of you know that some people don't get on the bus because you don't want to be inconvenienced? How many of you are talking to too many people? You need to get specific with your audience.

I wanted to make sure you understood that props are memorable, stand out and get your attention. If you can't get attention, you can't convert. These are things that you can make a movement with. We are here to create movements, and to give people a higher identity than the one they may have found you with.

Promise me that you will go to war against any mindset that you can't do what I'm about to teach you. The next time you go live, you do it because you are a movement maker and you won't be ready to go first because you are a prime mover.

Millions From The Stage - The Ultimate Secret To Captivating And Converting Your Audience With Props

We have hosted virtual and in-person events and we keep props to keep people's attention. In 2019, I had my first event. I wasn't even the best dressed there, but it never happened again. We had 10 people show up and I was so excited. At our second event, more people showed up. Don't despise small beginnings.

If one person shows up, you speak to them like it's one thousand. You can record it and put it on YouTube and thousands can watch it. Nothing is wasted when you have proof.

In 2020, this was our first 6 figure event. I went to an event, and my mentor was teaching. He made an offer for $15,000. I didn't even know this was possible, that you could go to an event, change someone's life and people are not mad they are being sold to.

In 2022, it was a $2.6M event. We used props in 2021 and this year the props got bigger. In 2023, there were less than 100 people there and it was another million dollar event. The same thing happened last year.

Why use Props?

You will not stand out by being boring and you should not be typical either.

How do you get started? Define your theory of the sale - why should they buy from you specifically?

This is simply you saying the premise of your offer. What is the one sentence that does that? When I attended trials as an attorney, we called it the theory of our case.

Comprehension objection list - Then you want to come up with a comprehension objection list. In trials, we had to come up with all the reasons why we would lose. Most people fail because they are afraid to look at why they might.

Define beliefs behind these objections.

Ensure there's a connection between the prop and the product. We are not playing with toys, we are using demonstratives to change lives.

Theory Of The Sales

Every (audience) need (solution) and solution

Example:

Every expert needs to be pitching their…

List all of their objections:

Money, trust, time, skepticism, fear, rejection, etc.

List the beliefs behind it - money - (I can't afford it)

When they say it's not the right timing, they are really thinking "I"ll do this later. This won't work for me, I already tried that."

Choose Your Props

Make sure there's a connection between the prop and the product. That prop is supposed to break down a belief they hold so they can get to their transformation.

Example:

I need a volunteer from the audience:

What is the name of your offer? Lead Booster Tool kit
Who does it serve? Entrepreneurs
What's the #1 outcome of your offer? Leads

Every entrepreneur needs leads and the Lead Booster Toolkit is the best solution because it helps you get leads in 30 days or less.

Objection list: Time

The belief behind that objection is this is not top priority for me.

Now we are coming up with the prop. I know when they say time, this isn't a top priority for them. So you want to get 24 of something. Every hour that you are not getting leads, your business is dying. How many days do you think your business can survive like this?

Show them every day their business does not have leads, it is dying. More importantly, they don't know it's dying so they don't know how long they have.

You can ask them, how many leads are you getting per hour?

What kind of props can you use?

- Easy - household items. There's been times where I used a bottle of water to show the transfer of belief.
- Make your own - I've used baskets from Etsy
- Ladder - showed the difference between a corporate ladder looking glittery and a business owner ladder looking dull, but it's really the opposite if you look harder
- Jail cell - if you have wrong beliefs, you are in an invisible prison

Time is not money, time is life. So when you don't invest in something you need, you are not saving money, you are wasting life.

Search for props in your house, on Instagram, or use Etsy.

If you DM me "Props" on Instagram, I will send you a link to an example of how I use props during a sales event.

Russell Brunson
One Funnel To Rule Them All

I always get asked what's the best funnel and the answer is…it depends. A lot of people mention how many funnels I have but there's only one funnel that matters in business.

"Properly exploited, one good idea that occurs to you while walking on a beach is worth more than 10 lifetimes of hard work" - Gary Halbert

We all have ideas, the idea is to properly exploit it and get it out to the world. A lot of people have ideas but don't execute them correctly. Over the last ten years, I don't think I was clear enough in my thinking behind it. Everything I've done is based on one funnel.

At the last FHL, I talked about the Linchpin framework. This is still the greatest business model on the planet.

For each business you start, you are just looking for one funnel to rule them all. Funnels are tools in a toolbox. The key is for your business specifically.

We launched ClickFunnels and I didn't know what that funnel would be. I funnel hacked other companies, and I launched with my first page. It looked like other SAAS companies. But most SAAS companies didn't know anything about internet marketing. So it didn't work.

After 5 times of trying, I didn't know how to sell ClickFunnels. No one wanted the free trial. It was frustrating for me. I remember talking to Mike Wilson, who was doing an event. He asked if I could speak at the event and asked me to sell ClickFunnels at the event.

I was trying to back out of it, it was a weekend event and it was streaming live. I had literally just built the perfect webinar and I built slides, then flew out to California. There were a couple hundred people in the room, made the offer for ClickFunnels and people started running to the back of the room. It caught me off guard and it was the first time I'd done it before.

Half the room was buying ClickFunnels and that night, we went to dinner and we were so excited. We actually made money from ClickFunnels and I knew how to sell it now.

The next step was to create a webinar and it was great. I was doing the webinar 2-3 times a week. I remember I did a webinar for Australia, it was 4 AM and there were 2 people on the webinar.

After the funnel is working, the next step is getting things to convert higher. One of the first things we found was where Todd had this idea to make a tiny tweak. This is what it takes to go from good to great.

Two weeks ago we held [Selling Online](#) and I took the offer and re-recorded a piece of the offer and then made 3X in sales.

So the tweak was on the sign up page to get a free ClickFunnels account, so they could see it before the webinar. 2,500 bought at the end, and 7,500 stuck with recurring.

After that, what are the other things we can tweak? It was frustrating when only 250 people would show up after 1,000 people registered. What can we do to get people to show up? We used these 3 indoctrination pages where there was a goal to get them excited about what would happen.

Someone just registered to learn about funnels, so I had this idea to have Chris & Mandy who worked for me design funnels and who would get it done quicker. People want to buy from people who show them fun along the way.

We had them battle in an Octagon, which was fun. Mandy was not a web designer and Chris was, and they competed against each other in the octagon building out their sales funnels.

So make it fun for people and get them excited to show up.

With all the other funnels, the only purpose is to get them into the webinar funnel. I launched DotCom Secrets, and the purpose was to get people to watch the webinar. I don't care about them actually buying books, I'm trying to get them into the one funnel that rules for me which is the webinar.

Thank You Page Webinar

What if we created a thank you page webinar? I plugged my webinar into the thank you page. Someone just bought Expert Secrets and on the page, I say your first training starts right now. They watch a 90 minute presentation and at the end they get an offer to buy a $97 ClickFunnels subscription.

You want to capitalize on their excitement immediately. The conversion rate isn't insane on this, but it does increase your average cart value.

The One Funnel Away Challenge

The goal was to get people to watch the webinar. People watched both me and Katelin Poulin pitch the webinar twice.

Then we started with front end offers. Steve Larson and I talked about doing dramatic demonstrations. We held the "Your First Funnel Launch" with a challenge and at the end we sold a package to ClickFunnels.

It's just a bunch of different ways to sell the same thing. For the ClickFunnels business, the one funnel that rules them all is the webinar.

But it depends on what the business model is. When I bought Dan's Magnetic Marketing business, I looked at what was working. They talked about the MIFGE - the Most Incredible Free Gift Ever and for me, I wasn't going to reinvent the wheel. So we made a new version of the MIFGE.

If you look at the Dan Kennedy business, everything is fueling towards this MIFGE funnel.

Then we are thinking, what are other dramatic demonstrations we can do? Tim Shields was in my Atlas group and he told me that I should go to Dan Kennedy's basement because marketing nerds want to see what that is. So I told Dan I wanted to come to his basement, we wrote the check and said let's go.

People registered for this dramatic demonstration which led into the MIFGE offer. 13,000 people registered and we went live from his basement. We had to bring Starlink in because Dan doesn't have internet. I remember asking him how he gets anything done. He's written 40 books and he's never been on Amazon.com. He asked me how do I get stuff done but it must be hard for me to focus.

So it was a big deal to bring the internet to Dan's basement. It was so fun and he took us into his bathroom, showed us his fax machine and people were going crazy in the comments.

We kept doing more fun things and everything leads back to the MIFGE funnel.

The Secrets of Success business is similar to Dan's business. We started adding upsells and downsells and drove traffic. From there, what are other dramatic demonstrations can we do? The first was the Think and Grow Rich challenge. The only goal is to get people to sign up for the Secrets of Success MIFGE.

The second challenge we did was we took one of the book sets and did a couple of interviews where we talked about the books. We did 3 calls and at the end we pitched the MIFGE.

Next we did a challenge called "Secrets of the Ages" with 3 live trainings which pushed them back to the MIFGE.

How many of you do podcasts? I wanted to interview Ryan Holliday. It was a really good interview and we called it Stoic Secrets and drove traffic to it. A podcast can become a dramatic demonstration. Then I paid Ryan to promote this to his list. We got tens of thousands of leads from that.

Prime Mover - we took our company and for tracking and accountability, we decided to break our coaching and software into two things. Inside Prime Mover, we have one funnel that moves them all and [Selling Online](#) is that funnel. What is the core thing you are selling inside your business? The thing we were selling is a $10K-$25K offer. For this, I knew I needed more time, so we needed a 3 day event.

If you don't want to do an event funnel, you can do a VSL funnel to a phone call. It depends on how you want to sell. I didn't want to be selling on phones so for me a 3 day event was the answer.

Bari Baumgartner is the best at this, so I bought her coaching program. I found the person who's the best in the world at it, gave her money and figured it out. I mapped out the structure of the event funnel, then we figured out the landing page for the offer. I funnel hacked probably 2 dozen event challenges too. I didn't copy one person, I took things from all these other people and built it out.

We have a $197 offer to be a fly on the wheel and watch or you can pay $497 to ask questions. Last August was the first one we did, and it was insane. The first time I launched this I didn't spend a lot on ads. We made money and used that money to reinvest in ads for round two. The first time you run the event is not about making money, it's about using that money to run the next one.

Some people ask if it's live or recorded and it's both. I love how I did certain pitches so some of them are being replayed and some of it is being done live, so I'm constantly tweaking it to make it better. It's just like how we launched the original ClickFunnels. We did the webinar, looked at the questions, tweaked the slides and did it over and over until eventually all of the presentations were flawless.

To increase show up rates, I made different videos for each of the sections that registered. A lot of people forget about it before the webinar, so I made videos leading up the event to get them excited. Our show up rate was increased by 50%. There's a set of videos for the VIPs that are different. I started bribing like crazy to make sure they would show up, and that little tweak got 70% to show up.

You have to consistently test and tweak incrementally. We just changed how we structured the offer. It got more people to come in and buy faster.

We went back to the Expert Secrets funnel, and someone buys the first upsell, they are also getting a ticket to the [Selling Online](#) event, so I'm weaving that in. Now all the book funnels drive traffic into my two core funnels - [ClickFunnels](#) and [Selling Online](#).

I want you to start thinking about that, getting that one funnel. Then you can start adding all these other funnels but the goal is to get them back to that one funnel. This is the difference.

Tim Shields

I'm going to show you how you can make money with auto webinars and the 4 step system that turns people from leads into paying customers.

I launched a new business on how to take beautiful landscape photos. I created a $27 product and sold it with Facebook ads. I worked hard to create a beginners course and this long sales page. I sold 10 units at $47 each and it was a complete failure. I wanted to give up and try something else.

I hired a coach and he told me I needed to create a webinar. I was petrified and listed a dozen reasons why I couldn't do it. I planned out every task on a whiteboard and we worked like dogs to create a webinar and new offer in 17 days. Suddenly the webinar started and I went live with Michael as my co-host. I sold a $297 masterclass which made $11K in sales.

With the replays, we got our sales to $34K. I delivered over the next 6 weeks live and I was overjoyed.

It wasn't what I was selling, it was the way I was selling it. 6 years later I've sold over 20,000 units through an automated webinar.

I've hosted webinars from all over the world and they have allowed my wife and I to travel all over the world, where we film ads, training content or webinars. We have sold over 47,000 masterclass bundles in total. Webinars are the best ways to sell digital products online.

What about challenges? It depends on the price of your offer. If your offer is between $200-$2K, webinars are perfect. A challenge is a webinar stretched over multiple days.

What is the secret of webinars?

Remember the movie Jerry McGuire - "You had me at hello"? This is what you want your prospects to say at the beginning. You do that through your origin story. You are leading toward pleasure or taking them away from pain.

At age 21, I was with my girlfriend Leah. She was about to go to her home country of Denmark. I was broke and had no idea how to raise the money to marry her, and then go to school full time. One day, we met with her cousin and her husband. I was working for a landscape company, and her cousin's husband told me his origin story.

1. I was trying to do "the thing". I had a job, I was broke,
2. I was failing and felt frustrated because I couldn't do the thing
3. I searched for a new and better way
4. I discovered the new way and created my own formula. I launched my own irrigation company
5. I experienced massive success after launching. I could pay for my tuition and all my living expenses. I was working 4 months a year in the summer
6. I felt so good! I no longer felt uncertain, I graduated from med school
7. I taught my formula to others who also experienced success

He had me at hello! His origin story completely hooked me. So I launched my irrigation business, and after running that company for 7 years, I sold it and we were able to buy our first house.

How did he ignite such a hot fire that motivated me? It was the power of the origin story. It works so well - follow me!

It's saying I found the way - follow me.

Good stories contain 2 steps.

1. First get them to believe one thing. This is the vehicle.
2. Second, present them with your fast and easy formula to get there - this is new opportunity

Most people get this wrong. Imagine you are Henry Ford and you are talking to horse and cart owners. Cars are way faster and you don't have to feed horses. After they believe they need a car, then you present them with your Ford Model T.

Bill Von Fumetti is teaching others how to do accounting. He sells a work from home bookkeeping offer. He gets you to believe a bookkeeping business is the vehicle. Once you believe that first thing, he comes in with the second punch, his program that fast tracks the launch of your bookkeeping business.

How do you get people to buy during a webinar?

1. Sign up
2. Show up
3. Watch until the end
4. Buy now

Sign up - tools to increase signups

- Give them a lead magnet
- Live giveaway of a physical product that your niche holds as valuable
- Promise a dramatic demonstration
- Lead them to pleasure - you will show them how to get the big results
- Promise to take away their pain that they are experiencing now

The lead magnet

Create a lead magnet that solves a real problem. It needs to be perceived as valuable. We have created checklists, and tools with amazing covers as lead magnets.

Convert your digital lead magnet into a physical product to increase the perceived value. We print photos of the cover of the lead magnet. We take that picture and tape it onto the front cover of an existing 6x9 book. I'll use that real book as a prop when shooting a video ad.

Example: 29 Landscape Secrets You Must Know

Upload the lead magnet to Amazon. Put a price of $20 and you can say in your ads, this book costs $20 on Amazon and you will get it free when you watch this workshop.

After the webinar is over, send them an email with a request for a review on Amazon.

Create a lead magnet with a cool image on cover. We used MidJourney then used Photoshop to put my head on the person.

Insert lead magnet into a graphic image that will be used in your advertising.

We make the email image look like a thumbnail image on YouTube.

After some clicks, they land on the opt in page. We remind them what they will get using the same image. They signed up but now they need to show up.

The next page is the confirmation page. I put a video on there telling people they will get free lead magnet and remind them they have a chance to win the giveaway product.

Send them email and text reminders:
- 4 days out
- 3 days out
- 2 days out
- Day before live event

Day of live event

- 5:30 am
- One hour before
- 15 minutes before (straight text only email)

Day of webinar - customers land on the countdown page. Put a video there so people have something to watch. Remind them about the free lead magnet again.

How to get people to watch until the end? As soon as the webinar starts within the first minute, show them a slide of the free lead magnet, and tell them they have to watch live because I will verbally tell them the link. They won't get it by email.

Next I remind them to keep watching because the live giveaway is coming up. Make sure to drop names in chat to win.

Show them the lead magnet:

- During the first minute
- After the origin story
- Right before the pitch

Set the hook continually in the end to end webinar SLIDE

How do you get them to buy?

Unexpected bonus - this is where you have pitched your offer and you save your most valuable bonus. Say you were going to be selling it on its own but my team convinced me to include it today.

Read out the names of people who have bought programs during the live webinar. I want to congratulate this person and this person, etc.

How do you make older masterclasses make money? I have 10 auto webinars that I promote.

- Scheduled auto webinars
- Advertise with email
- Each webinar has its…

Track each link in your buyer's chain. Take a look at subject line, how many clicks, etc. Each link can be strengthened. This strategy brings in ⅔ of annual revenue.

Without cold traffic, you have nothing. You need to be able to buy traffic. Let's say you have a $10 optin rate for webinar registrations. If you have an 8% purchase rate, you will get 20 sales.

What if you doubled the price of your offer to $997? Now you'll have a 2X time ROAS.

Expensive offers support paid traffic but low ticket offers do not. For low ticket, market to your email list.

After you pitch, say I'm going to answer questions, then you have 20 slides. Each slide has an objection and you answer that by telling a story about someone who had the same objection and it worked. Do this instead of answering questions live from chat.

You can get my free cheat sheet here on how to create your own Dramatic Demonstration Webinars that sell: LaptopLife.com

Josiah Grimes

I was reading Dotcom Secrets, and at this point I was pretty young. The first thing I did was in real estate, but the way I'd make it in marketing was with VSLs. Today we've done over 9 figures in VSL sales.

VSL funnels are like broken iPhones - they can be pretty jacked up and still work.

2 Important Zones

1. You have the happy zone where you are making more money than spending on ads
2. Sad zone where you are not

When people say VSL, they are expecting a video that sets an appointment for a sales team.

My first rule is to listen to whatever Russell says, and my second rule is to do a bazillion split tests.

We took all of the 5 biggest wins and pieced them together which allows us to develop the most dope sauce VSL funnel of all time.

3 Big Questions

1. When should I use a VSL?
2. What is the best framework working right now?
3. Where are benchmarks for VSL conversions in 2025?

Each step has a conversion metric. You need to know what the benchmark is. For example, if your landing page is converting at 9%, should you be focused that you're not closing at 20%? No, you should fix the landing page.

When to use a VSL?

- To break in an offer before going 1 to many
- Price point requires over $5K that requires a personal touch
- When you want to make lots of dollars

VSL Framework

- Pain Point - lots of people are trying this, but they should be doing this or you will fail
- Your motivation - people want to know why you are about to tell them your secrets, it's because we all win together
- Credibility - why should they listen to you
- Likability - why should they like you, humanizes you, you are a parent, or a joke
- Who is this case study for - for anyone that wants to improve their golf swing for example
- Market factors - this is why right now is the moment you need to take action
- How you earn the solution - how much did it cost you?
- Intro Your solution - you can't tell them what it is, just the name. It needs to be something they can't search and find, You need a unique mechanism
- Demarket - separate your solution from others. Tell them what yours is not. You might be thinking this is X but it's actually different
- 3 secrets - these are secrets, not components
- Recap their pain points without a solution
- List the benefits - if you use this, you get all these things
- Future pace them - if you don't have these pain points, would you be successful?
- Qualify - who this is not for
- Call to action - book a call
- Requalify them
- Sign them up

Conversion Percentage Benchmarks

Ads to landing page, most people are running omni channel advertising. The conversion between ad and landing page should be 2.5%
Landing page to VSL conversion - 25%
Schedule page - 25%
Application page - 60%
Show up - 75%
Book a call - 65%
Sale - 8%

Basic metrics when we sell something between $5-$10,000

What's the most important metric for VSLs? On webinars be careful about ROAS. In VSL funnels, because there's a lag between when they book a call, we have to care about cash. In the VSL world, C-ROAS is key.

The Most Dope Sauce Funnel of All Time

We did both easy and hard split tests. We found if we took the winning components and pieced them together, it made the highest converting funnel.

We call this the Frankenstein funnel. They all fall under one concept which means being hyper personalized. We have AI now, and how do we optimize what's on the other side of this funnel?

Biggest Win #1

We run a quiz funnel with marketing qualifying questions that are built into the survey.

The second big part is we go to an IVSL which gives them the answers to the quiz and it asks them to sort themselves for a free lead magnet.

Next is a free, avatar specific ebook opt in
Then we get them to Melissa for data verification

From that, they get their avatar specific mini course. They select which mini course they would like. They have to reply to our email in order to access the mini course.

We ask: What state are you in? What type of real estate have you done? That helps our mail servers. The ones that do reply are more qualified, nurtured and purchased. By the time they get to the end of the mini course, we have a complete profile for them.

Choose your own adventure - as they choose certain things, they get different email sequences. Now we have 3 main tracks: newbie, entrepreneur and veteran. Those emails push them to the mini course. Before they book a call, we are lead scoring them.

Leadscoring is a little hard. The concept is you want the highest quality leads going to the reps that can close them. That correlates with success and that's how you score points.

If you look at the sales motion, we make sure we send email, text and after that you have your triage call, then sending them to the closer. There's a precall again, a nurture discovery call and then the close.

Russell Brunson & Todd Dickerson
State of the Union

We have two things to show you:

1. All the cool things happening inside the platform
2. One of our favorite features called Frameworks

ClickFunnels + OfferLab

Andrew Culver - I lead an incredible team we've built that gets the idea from Russell and Todd's heads onto the platform. We're here to connect you with the right people if you are having issues running your business. With OfferLab, if you've been in the payment space, there's just some things you can't do. Sometimes we limit our opportunities, but if you ask the right questions, sometimes you find out that we can do this now.

These guys identified a bearer to the entry to entrepreneurship 10 years ago that would help people. You needed a funnel but you couldn't just build a funnel so one of the core things was that you can do it without a developer. We take it for granted now, that's a rare opportunity in one's career.

I've built a ton of products, but it's very rare to be the first person in the world to bring a new technology to market. So you heard a lot about OfferLab and it's an honor for me to be part of that journey.

I want to paint a different picture. The story you heard is the need for this platform to exist. If you understand everything we talked about yesterday, you see we introduced a product that brings entrepreneurs together. But there's a big piece that we didn't talk about yesterday. I want to paint a whole other picture of not just a platform that brings people together. It's not just about ClickFunnels. It's about this mission of this company, the thing that drives us to create as many entrepreneurs as possible.

We meet these people all the time. So this platform doesn't only bring people together. We are going to bring an entire industry together. You saw how you can bring your offer from all these other platforms into OfferLab and they are now available for other people to sell. There's the ability to take offers you have found on OfferLab and when you are approved to promote them, you can ask for their permission to sell them in your funnel.

We have this button that says "Add from Zendrop" which is a platform to add products into your ClickFunnels account. Then the third bridge that says "Add from OfferLab". You come to the marketplace, see something you want to sell, ask for permission, you are approved and you see a link that says sell on ClickFunnels. Now you can sell it directly, put it in a funnel as an upsell, etc.

You can go in now and edit the price and sell it for as much as you want. You can offer this product for less if you have something on the backend that compensates for it. When that product is sold, that order gets processed and it gets fulfilled from anywhere. It could be on Shopify or anywhere. We have brought ClickFunnels interconnection into the other platforms.

OfferLab will fill this gap to sit at the city square of all of internet marketing.

Zendrop is this marketplace with over 1.5M products. OfferLab is a new marketplace and you can import those offers and start selling. Now you can sell other people's products inside your funnels.

One way to think about this is, it's the ClickFunnels affiliate now, powered by OfferLab. It's ClickFunnels integrated offers. You can go to OfferLab, find an order bump for your funnel, import it into your account and start selling immediately.

This is closer to what you think of as drop shipping. You are buying products at wholesale and turning it around and selling it at a price that the seller allows.

If you have your own offer, and you want to increase your average cart value, that's what OfferLab is for. You can also put your products into OfferLab for others to sell.

If you don't want to build a continuity program, sell mine. As you get deeper into our world, you will see the power of it and it will change everything.

What if you want to run your own affiliate program? The affiliate app inside ClickFunnels is included inside your basic account. You can have a form that someone can sign up as an affiliate. You can modify the commission and sign people up based on workflows inside ClickFunnels. You can customize the dashboard, and you have full analytics. This includes things such as CPA, dynamic commissions, and second tier commissions.

One hack we are using now to create viral funnels. They get their account, sign up and on the thank you page, we tell them if you want to become an affiliate, you can. We put the link on the thank page and there's no barriers so they can start making sales instantly.

One of our goals is to create an integrated platform and we've partnered with Zapier. You can click "Add to Zapier" and see all the apps.

One of our core things we've focused on is how we get higher conversions.

- Faster checkout
- Expand payment methods
- More international support
- Apple pay
- Partnership with Link
- Stripe is now native on the platform

Link enables us to partner and use billing profiles from OpenAI and other networks. They can buy from you without having to enter their credit card number.

There's over 100 payment methods that are enabled by this. When they tested this, they saw an increase of 46% in sales.

Stripe

Click Stripe path in ClickFunnels. Put your email in for the pilot program as we are rolling it out slowly, over the next quarter.

- Support One to Many Presentations
- Connect your Webinars
- Connect your meetings
- Inside your workflow automations

We are adding a Zoom integration into your workflows.

Survey Workflows

Survey Funnels - you can build a survey workflow and use it in multiple places inside your account. Install the workflow app, add a question, you can add all sorts of filters, and then you can set if you want to store that information on a contact's record for later. So you can do conditional splits based on anything they do in real time.

Inside of your survey you can split and branch based on what they answered. You drop the survey element on that page, tell them which logic to use behind the scenes. People answer the questions in real time and it's super fast.

Stores, Zendrop & Add to Cart

Inside stores, if you don't have physical products to sell, you can click "add from Zendrop" and you can get started for free. They have millions of products. Select the products you want to sell, and it tells you what the fulfillment cost is. Then you sync it into your account or you can print on demand and customize it however you like.

You can literally create your own swag store in 5 minutes. It's not just funnels, we are also supporting "add to cart". It'll pull in the product details and let people check out. Now you are not pushing people from platform to platform.

You can also create a miniature workflow, and decide what happens when people enroll, right from the lightning bolt. Our courses by default allow you to present your videos in a simple way. You have a beautiful membership area right out of the box and it's fully mobile responsive. It has comments in your community as well.

Anything you can dream on in a course, we're now able to do. If you want to drop your top 10 videos, you can get a style and upgrade your simple course into a complex course by applying a design.

Communities - you can interact with the team. These communities sit right beside the courses and you can give people to different groups and communities inside your account when they purchase. It's all in one clean seamless place and they can access it at any time.

Barnum PT - free chrome plugin which is the ultimate funnel hacker tool. I use this 30 times a day and grab things for my swipe file. We have Barnum AI coming up soon as well, and it makes your funnel hacking journey so much easier.

We also have:
Two factor authorization
AI store builder powered by Zendrop
Quick Actions

API Access - have your developers look at what's possible
Frameworks

Share Funnels - this is one reason why our affiliate program grew so big. Over the last 10 years we've had over 200 people win a dream car. We cover the monthly payment, everything from lambos to minivans and everything in between. We've paid out over $162M in affiliate commissions over the last decade from promoting ClickFunnels.

Frameworks is the next step up. Imagine this:

- You create a website
- A store
- And 3 funnels
- A course
- And a killer follow up funnel

Add the frameworks app to your account

It takes that and presses that into a framework. You give someone that link and it copies it into their ClickFunnels account, so you can share it. You partner with us and you can have software that's customized for your business inside ClickFunnels.

I gave people 6 frameworks for free when they upgraded their account. We built out an entire ecomm store, with 300 products. The site is called Startup Drugz which was white label. That was one framework where they could customize their designs.

Framework #2 - membership site - 30+ funnel templates. Then I took mine and the Dan Kennedy training and we gave them the funnel and site.

Frameworks 3-6 are software products.

Do you see how this can work for you? How many of you have heard about Sam Brannan. He realized during the gold rush, that he was going to sell picks and shovels. He put them in this store, and everyone wanted to pan for gold. So they all bought his tools and he became the first millionaire in San Francisco's history.

Let's say you are a gym owner and you have your own frameworks. Now, you can take these frameworks and sell them to other gym owners. Or maybe you are a life coach. You created a course, and an entire framework that runs your entire business. You can take that, put it into ClickFunnels and sell to other life coaches.

Frameworks allow you to white label, license, and sell your best funnels.

Our #1 affiliate builds out stores and gives them away for free. Build a few stores in ClickFunnels and give them away for free.

Prince EA

They call Las Vegas the city of sin. I'm a word guy and that word sin is interesting and it means to miss your mark. The greatest sin is to not be who you came here to be.

Arthur Berry was a very charming man who lived in the 1920s. He was one of the most world renowned thieves. He stole over $100M in jewelry but he only stole from wealthy people. Until one day he got caught and got thrown in prison. He stayed there for 18 years.

After he served his sentence, he moved to a small town in New England and lived a quiet life. But after a month, the people recognized him and reporters came to interview him. They asked him who would he say he stole the most from? Arthur replied it was himself.

He said I could've been a teacher, a business owner or anything worthwhile but instead I spent ⅔ of my life in prison. So I tell this story because I think we all have a lot of Arthur inside of us. That fear that robs us of who we came here to be.

There are 207 million content creators worldwide and 127 million influencers.

Out of that there are 4 million who will be considered leaders in their niche. That might seem like a big number but that's only 2%.

Let me ask you one question: what do Charles Manson and Warren Buffett have in common? They were both star students of Dale Carnegie's program How To Win Friends And Influence People.

There's 4 frogs sitting on a log. One jumps off. How many frogs on that log? The answer is 4. Just because you decide to do something doesn't mean you do it. Don't let your knowledge stay being knowledge. Ideas without labor are stillborn. So take imperfect action.

I started out working part time doing odd jobs and my boss said being a creator was a pipe dream, but I kept going. I used to work at Walgreens and my first videos got no views. I worked so hard and studied so much, then boom - there was one video that changed everything. I felt like I'd cracked the code.

Pretty soon I started getting attention. Oprah reached out and invited me to her show. You are one video away from a new destiny.

So I took everything I learned and decided to teach it with people who want to make a difference in this world. There's a creator, Joshua who told me I motivated him to start YouTube.

Another creator messaged me that he watched this video 3 years ago. Today I'm going to hit a million subs.

I share those stories because it works.

1. If you want to stand out in your industry, you have to be a confident contrarian. There's never been a statue erected for conformity.

Dan Kennedy said look what everyone else is doing and do the opposite. That stuck with me. The world class people know the rules so you can break them effectively. You need to stand out, and you need to understand how the brain works.

It's about understanding psychology and how the brain operates. When the brain is triggered with novelty, we can use it for the good of the world. You need to look, sound different and your energy needs to be different.

What are you saying that's dramatically different, maybe even opposite? This is how you stand out.

One of my favorite examples is Patagonia. During the Black Friday sale, they put an ad out saying don't buy this jacket, and their sales spiked by 30%.

2. Deliver a Bold Message

Be bold and mighty forces will come visit your aide. It's not what you say, it's how you say it. It's all about delivering. You know the algorithm rewards boldness.

People are persuaded more by the depth of your conviction than the height of your logic. People like Russell, Donald Trump, Oprah, Andrew Tate, and Alex Hormozzi - what do all have in common? They all have bold tastes, are not afraid to pick a side, are not afraid to turn some people off and are not afraid to have attention.

They don't just communicate, they connect. They stimulate emotions. Fortune favors the bold.

3. Stop Being Original

Jim Jones says "Nothing is original. Steal from photos, dreams, trees, bodies of water. Select only things that speak directly to your soul. Don't bother concealing your thievery.

"It's not what you take things from, it's where you take them to". - Jon Luc Goddard

The biggest creators, don't create. They:

- Investigate
- Validate
- Iterate

They reverse engineer and model success.

Isaac Newton: *"If I have seen further, is it by standing on the shoulders of giants."*

When I met Tony Robbins for the first time, I remember he said nothing I'm about to tell you, I invented. Everything I'm about to tell you I learned from someone else. Success leaves clues.

When it comes from your content creation, it's about proven ideas.

4. The 2% Obsess Over Their Ideas

Example - say you are a dentist and your audience is people looking for teeth whitening. Go to YouTube, the 2nd largest search engine in the world, type "dentist how to" and you see it populates what people are searching for.

Then you rank by view count, and now you have ideas for viral videos. I've created videos with millions of views doing this.

During your investigation when you find videos on channels with lower subscribers but with a ton of views, that's when you find gold.

This is the process MrBeast and Alex Hormozzi does and you should as well.

5. Maintain Relevance

You need to stay relevant and timely. MrBeast's biggest video was the squid games videos and he jumped on that when it was at its peak. Timing is the biggest variable, and if you get it right, a small channel can get a big reach. Use Google analytics and X.

Look at what's happening at this moment and what current audiences love. In the middle is the sweet spot. If you hit that sweet spot, you will get authority.

You have the ideas, but they are nothing without this next thing. Before I tell you what it is, there's a war going on and we're all on the battlefield. The 2% are 5 star generals in this war of attention.

6. The Art of Capturing Attention

The most valuable currency is attention.

Your attention is worth $816 a day and in 10 years $2.5M. The biggest mistake I see creators make is this…imagine you go to a 5 star restaurant. You order your steak, and the steak comes on a cheap paper plate. This is exactly what creators do. They put so much attention into the content, that their packaging is trash.

Your title and thumbnail is 50% success of your video. You need to come up with the thumbnail and title before you shoot the video.

The purpose of good packaging is to get the click or stop the scroll. That's the only reason because 75% of views come from recommendations.

You want to create curiosity. Don't just make them click on their video, you have to make it so that they can't not click. Make it so simple that a 7 year old can understand it.

Don't use clickbait. That will ruin the satisfaction score. The thumbnail has to be in the same world as the video.

Color - contributes up to 90% of the judgement or products.

Words on thumbnails outperform thumbnails without words. Just put a few power words.

Blue is a powerful color. One of my biggest videos has a blue thumbnail. MrBeast uses blue thumbnails.

Another big hack is to put numbers in your title.

Put your face on the thumbnail with text.

Transformational - before and after images

Think and Grow Rich wasn't the original title. Napoleon Hill was trying to figure out what to call the book. The book publisher called him and told him they were going to call it "How To Use Your Noodle To Make A Boodle."

So before he went to sleep he asked his subconscious mind to come up with a million dollar book title. At 3AM he woke up with the title and that book went on to sell millions of copies.

You have 1.8 seconds to grab attention with a title.

- Does it create curiosity?
- Does it create conflict?
- Does it start a conversation?

7. The Art of Engagement

Customers need at least 7 hours of access, 11 touchpoints in at least 4 locations to buy.

A lot of creators who create long form content are crushing it. That's how you meet that 7 hour rule. Watch time is everything. It's how you turn views into customers. It increases your authority in your niche and you can convert parts of it into short form.

You need to tell stories. These are older than written language. Storytellers in every culture were always revered. Tell better stories than your competitors and you will win.

Storytelling Structure

- Hook
- Body
- Payoff

Hook - you got to start it off with a shocking question, statement or story.

Example: When given the choice between being blind or being deaf, do you know what most people choose?

Did you know the average person spends 4 years of his life looking down at his cell phone?

Do you know the day of the week you are most likely to die from a heart attack?

Body - you need to leave breadcrumbs, do not give the payoff too soon.

Example: "There's one sport that if you play, will reduce your chance of dying by 70%..."

In that video, I used props which are visual metaphors. It's a great way to get more views. There's something about holding something. I also found that wearing glasses converts more too. These little things can make a big difference.

A mistake I made - I did a short video which got 46M views, but the graph was flat in the beginning then it went up. In shorts, every second counts. I went to the end of the video, went to the back end on YouTube and trimmed that point off where I said Thanks guys.

8. Stay In Your Lane

Do not make content outside of your niche because you attract an audience that will ruin your reach. If your audience doesn't resonate because you brought them in from some other type of content, YouTube will not send your content up.

9. Identity > Belief

If you don't change your identity, nothing will change. Belief can move movements, but often it's not strong enough and people snap back. Changing your identity is the most important quality for authority.

There's a Dad who wants to watch a game and he finds a picture of a world map. He cuts it into pieces and tells his son that if he can solve the puzzle, he'll play with him, buy ice cream and buy his favorite toy. He's thinking it will take a long time, but a few minutes later the son comes back with a completed puzzle. The Dad said how did you figure this out so fast? The boy said on the back of the map there was a picture of a man's face and I knew if I got the man right, then the world would come together.

Psycho Cybernetics by Maxwell Maltz is one of my favorite books. He was a plastic surgeon and found after he worked with his patients, they still felt ugly. He realized there was the self image involved too.

There's 2 ways to change your identity - visualization and action.

10. Servant Leaders

The 2% is service obsessed.

"You can have everything you want in life if you just help enough people get what they want" - Zig Ziglar

There's a story of a Mom and a son. The son is angry at the Mom and runs outside. He tells his Mom he hates her but he hears an echo back "I hate you". So he runs back in and says there's a mean boy outside that says he hates me.

She says go tell him you love him, so he goes back outside and says I love you. What you send out, you will get back.

11. Love - The Greatest SuperPower

At the Washington Olympics, there were 9 contestants at the starting line of the 40 yard dash. Bang - they were off. Everyone ran and one boy tripped in the beginning, fell down and started to cry. The other 8 heard the boy's cries, looked back and turned back. One little girl bent over, kissed him and said "this will make it better". Then all 9 held hands and crossed the finished line together. The people in the crowd cheered for 10 minutes.

We know that winning means nothing unless we get there together.

CreatorJourney.com

Stu McClaren
5 Proven Keys To Million Dollar Launches

August 17, 2004 - do you know where you were? I was living in Fulton, MS working for my mentor. We were living in a ranch house and on that day, I could not wait to spend $1,000 - more money I'd ever spent on a training program before - and the moment I had a chance to buy, I didn't hesitate.

It was because of John Reese. He was the creator of a product called Traffic Secrets. You might not know him but you have benefited. On that day, he generated $1M with a product launch in less than 24 hours.

The day after he released a report to detail what happened. He mentioned a guy named Jeff Walker. He wrote the bestseller Launch.

A year later, Jeff came out with his own course which I bought and studied. Fast forward and Russell and I launched a product, Affiliate Inferno. We generated close to half a million dollars and I knew launches worked.

Since 2016, I've continued to refine and practice to get better and better with this one skill. Now our launch range is from $3.35 to $9.2 million dollars.

We've been teaching others to do the same. Like Matt Diamante who owns an SEO agency. He made:

$3K a month during launch 1
$16K with launch 2

Alex Kincacid made $700K. She took up painting, and earned this with her most recent launch.

Another client made $317K selling educational resources.

There's often this thought of launches vs funnels - who will beat who in the end? But launches can be friends with funnels and you can do amazing things together.

Launches can fuel funnels and are better together.

The success of your launch is depending on two things:

1. Traffic
2. Conversions - you have to convert people who are interested into paying customers

You need to create a long runway. The bigger your runway, the longer your results.

For example, it took me 7 years to convince my wife I was the man of her dreams, but it's been my most successful launch ever.

You need to build up excitement and anticipation

1. Connection
2. Awareness
3. Launch - May 12 - this is the date that the desire phase begins. This is when most typical launches are framed out. During that I'm sharing the opportunity, on what I call the first step someone needs to take, and I share a piece of content of giving people a high level overview of the outcome they are after
4. The next step - for me, a webinar where I make the offer
5. Buy phase - the cart closes 4 days later
6. Wow phase - the most important phase - the delivery of whatever they purchased is like the pre-launch to whatever you want to offer next

If you want a business that lasts, over deliver, take care of people and create an amazing experience.

In Chapter 30 of [my latest book](), I go over the details on these 4 things.

1 - Pick a Launch date

Craft messaging that resonates - this creates instant trust with your audience.

We do it by answering "How will life be better or different after purchasing your offer?"

2 - We write short phrases that describe their now world and contrast that to their future world.

Your audience feels seen, heard and understood which creates trust. That sets the stage for what you want to offer.

Describe their now world better than they can.

3 - Choose the right launch style

- Coaching week
- Challenge launch
- JV launch
- Summit launch
- Internal launch

Find the ones that are right for you.

Launch elements - affiliates, social media, video, ads,

It can be overwhelming, so just pick a few things.

I focused on having a great video, writing the sales letter and I leverage my experience working with affiliates. With my emails, it was probably a C+. But with each one, I spend time making it better. Don't go into it, grow into it. We are playing the long game.

This is the first launch that leads to the next one, and so on.

Refer to Chapter 31 of my book - finding your launch style.

4 - Install belief in your offer

People will not buy from you because they don't believe in you. Or they won't buy from you because they don't believe in themselves.

If you want to create belief in you, you have to create social proof.

I look for headlines that are not me saying you should do this, but headlines that give social proof of what I'm saying is valid. So I look for articles that demonstrate what I'm saying is valid. It's Forbes, Netflix, Apple and the NY Times demonstrating this.

The way you create belief in your process is through case studies.

Bonny Snowden teaches people how to draw animals. She made a video where she talked about how she went from $0 to a $1M membership in two years. You can build an incredible business in a tiny niche business.

Ali Kay has an evergreen funnel and had 1,400 members over 2 years.

With one launch she welcomed 3,000 new members. She was so excited, and it ended up being a $1.6M launch in the art space.

Do something in your launch designed to give people a quick win.

When your audience believes it's possible for them, it's inevitable they will buy. We want our people saying "I can do this" and feeling it.

5 - Find leverage for big results.

The success of your launch is dependent on

1. Traffic
2. Conversions

One of the best ways to get traffic is through affiliates. You can find them here, through OfferLab and through your customers.

Matt Donaldson

No one knows who I am but I bet every one of you has clicked on my ads. I'm from Liverpool. I started doing this in the 90s and I had Crohn's disease at the time, but I'm doing very well now. I had a very technical background and I realized that I could combine the power of tech and drive an insane amount of traffic.

Today I spend 8 figures a year running traffic to large scale events where we average one million attendees.

I see a lot of people leaving money on the table.

I work with people like Tony Robbins, Russell Brunson and Matthew McConaughey. It's easy to put the spotlight on me because I run all the traffic for these events.

The Traffic Mindset Shifts

Traffic platforms give you the tools but the real advantage comes from how you use them. Do the same as everyone else you'll get the same results

Go Long

- Events need attention spans
- Long ads - a higher show up rate
- Build lookalikes from the 95% viewers - Facebook gives you the ability to see who interacts with your content

On Facebook you can build an audience from people who watch 95% of any video, and you know they likely have a longer attention span. Show static ads to those what watch 95% of the video but didn't sign up.

Launch Insights

Find new users, new domains, new pixels (try not using the same pixel for every product you sell). I've tested this and for every new event, use a new domain name and a new pixel because that forces Facebook to find new people. The problem with new domains is they don't have Google history. Add your domain to the Google console as soon as possible.

Get ranked quicker hack - when you launch a new site, and you run ads on Facebook, you build hype and people search for that event on Google. If you are not there, you will miss sales, so you can go to Fiverr and pay a bunch of people to search for your website and click on it. That tells Google it must be relevant.

Don't just focus on buyers, buy cheap chat hype to boost the energy of the event. They will fill those chat rooms and be hyped, and the activity in the chat will hype up the event.

Use a reminder event and show them to everyone that signed up.

Use the red dot. Look at the things you've been conditioned to recognize. We've always been used to the red dot. When you run the ads, run them directly to your leads.

Protect Your Momentum

- Every launch has its obstacle
- Any downtime can kill momentum
- Use AI to find cheaper interest buckets

When we were running the Matthew McConaughey ad, Facebook ended up giving us a problem. Eventually they fixed the issue, the ads came back on, but the lead costs were triple what they were. I had to think outside the box. At the time, ChatGPT was new and it revealed something to find cheaper leads.

Anyone who posts positive comments, and likes it, you should stalk their profile. Get as much info as you can find. Go on LinkedIn, and create a Google doc about them. I did this for this launch, and I had pages of likes, interested and fed it to AI and asked it to find the common threads of these people. When I did this, my costs went way down again. It's because people are bidding, and all these people are signing up for your event. With Tony Robbins' launch last month, I was running ads to people who liked romance novels.

Users will always google your pitched product name. Ensure you are in the search results. Neglecting this will lose you a significant amount of sales.

Things That Are Working Well

- 1X1 square for videos over 20s = cheaper CPL
- 9x16 for videos under 30 seconds

- 16x9 and 1x1 for cinematics ads
- Minimal edited videos with just simply subtitles
- Show status ads to people who watch 95%.
- Open your Facebook ad copy with "Breaking NEWS"
- Use "reach" or awareness campaigns for your LIVE NOW ads - higher showup rates
- Make a static ad with "Last chance" or Final notice" for cheaper leads
- This is gold in WorldWide audiences with purchase intent (exclude Africa and Asia)
- Run close down static ads with the text "Event Only Offer"

Hala Taha

Imagine starting a podcast in your car because you had no mic, equipment, nor idea what you were doing? All you knew was to just start. That led you to 100M downloads and you became one of the most famous podcasters in the world.

This happened to my client. She did have a skill which was photography. She started a photography wedding business but she felt lonely. She dreamed of starting a podcast. But some doubts crept in. She didn't have a good place to record but she promised to do it for 90 days. Those 90 days turned into 9 years and a multi million dollar empire. Her name is Jenna Kutcher and it all started with a podcast.

Who can relate to her? You don't know how to grow or monetize your audience?

I'm the CEO and founder of YAP media and I used to be like you, dreaming of building a personal brand. 6 years ago I launched my podcast and today I'm a top 10 podcast on Apple. I've helped hundreds of people and brands grow their business and I'm going to teach you how to do it today.

Podcasts are no longer audio only. It's a show and it's mainstream now. You might think they are over-saturated. But why are already successful entrepreneurs investing in podcasts?

It's because of their personal brand. They understand this is the most valuable asset. It creates a moat around your business. Long form content builds credibility. When you become a podcaster, you become a creator entrepreneur and you unlock unlimited ways to monetize.

How much time do you have to commit? It's a long game.

You can own or buy

- If you are fit for the buy path - you have money to invest
- You want more customers and lead gen
- You don't have the desires to invest time in creating content
- You might not want to share your face

Ways To Buy

Commercials - programmatic ads

- Reach your audience at scale
- Control your messaging
- Host reads ads targeted at a specific audience
- Work with a podcast agency
- Higher conversion rate
- Better listener experience

Higher cost
Limited scale

CMP based pricing
Cost per 1,000 impressions
Programmatic 5-18
Host read 20-35

YAP pricing example for monthly host read DAI flight

My CPM is $28
$12,600 to buy an ad across 30 days

Branded content - sponsored on your podcasts

Anything outside of your podcast commercials
Usually it includes 360 pricing

$30-$250 ECPM or more
Cost across all of the platforms

The pricing is based on:

- The channels selected for the campaign
- Level of effort and customization required
- How niche or desirable the audience is
- Track record of show
- Value of personal endorsement from podcaster

Example:

Opus Clip - AI editing software

This is a faceless campaign and I represented Opus Clip.

You can buy your audience via commercials or branded content to recap.

You can own your podcast

You have value to share
You put your face out there
You are willing to share your content

Start, monetize & grow

When it comes to starting, pick a target audience and go for it. Don't overthink it. It's the consistency that will build it. It can take 2 years or more before you see any ROI.

Your podcast should evolve from the way you title it, to the way you format it.

Tech

- Simplecast - hosting provided
- Riverside - recording

Monetize

- Sell your own products/services
- Sponsorships
- Guest networking

How much money can I make on sponsorships?

3 variables to maximize monetization

- Impressions
- Ad slots
- CPM

10-15 min of content per ads is a good rule of thumb.
Typically you'll work with a network for ads and they take 30%

$12,600 x 6 ad slots = $75,600

If my show is ten minutes long, I can only put 1 ad, I'm 6Xing my revenue by having a longer show.

Last year there was an IOS update. My average CPM was $28. My payout was $52K/month. 74% came from commercials and 26% came from branded content.

So my total revenue was $622,707.

What if I told you how I made $6M? Guest Networking. When Covid hit, I had more time and my agency took off. I reserve podcast slots for guests who provide value and who also might need my LinkedIn help.

My email signature includes information about my company. I sent my guest a branded box with a gift. I mention it during the conversation and my guests end up pitching me by the end. Then it leads to a call. Most of the people end up becoming my clients.

Lori Harder, Host of Earn Your Happy was interviewing a woman and asked her to critique her pitch deck. The next day it led to an investment in her company. Your guests can become clients, mentors or investors and it's a powerful strategy.

Design a podcast that will fuel your business goals. If you are able to create in a way that's interesting, you can get podcastors to sell your own products.

<u>Grow It</u>

1. 50% promotion / 50% production
2. Good content leads to word of mouth
3. Be visible where podcast listeners are, advertise in the player apps, guest on competitor podcasts
4. Diversity in your funnels

PSO - podcast search optimization - have same keywords in your metadata over and over
Video funnels - you need a video element to promote your podcast on social media
DM Funnels - you need to spoon feed your link to grow followers

Email funnel - grow your list and email them for every new episode
Apple and Spotify chart - daily new subscribers

Years ago, I was fired from working with a DJ. I was Hala from Hot 97 but I was crushed. So I got dreaming and started a blog. I wanted to empower other women in the entertainment industry. The DJs were now asking me to host at their parties. MTV reached out and they wanted us to have a reality TV show. I thought I'd finally made it but two weeks before they launched it, they told me they were not going to run with it.

At this point, I thought I'm never going to make it. So I got my MBA, went into corporate. Then an opportunity came and I wasn't chosen. I decided this was the last time that someone was going to control my future. I decided I'd lead millions online with my YAP podcast. This was 2018 and I thought with my radio and marketing experience, I could do this too.

Everyone told me I was crazy, but I just started. My main focus for promotion was LinkedIn and by episode 8, I had 20 volunteers who helped me grow my brand for free. Within two years, we topped the charts and are on track to make 8 figures. Podcasts gave me my dream career and dream team.

The creator economy is just beginning and it's not too late. You just need to start.

Dr. Sonja Stribline

I don't train ballerinas or princesses, I only train warriors. Let's imagine you are in a room with multi-millionaires and billionaires but more than anything, you're in a room with your people. How do you show up then?

I believe I'm the newest person to this community. I met Russell 6 months ago. When I saw Tony's, Russell's and Dean's ads, I thought someone was missing from this ad. I didn't see a representation from a female. Then I saw a young woman on there and I wanted to comment. I didn't comment. So I made it my business to get into the room and show up differently.

How many of you came here to look for something more? How many of you want to tap into the legacy of what you want to leave for your family?

You can say the thing but your actions will not lie.

The two most important days of your life: the day you were born and the day you die. I say it's the day you are born and the day you figure out what your true purpose is in life.

Many of us are trying to figure out what our purpose is. I believe those that really want to take action join communities that are successful.

I've never been a part of a community like this in my life, outside of the U.S. Army. A decade ago, I was done with this world. So I made a decision that I was going to take my life, but the only reason I didn't was that I knew my son would come home and find me. I know there's at least one person here that came to get your life saved.

Some of you want more strategy, some of you want more tactics but I believe that what you really need is to get rid of the old version of you. At 15 years old, I had my first child. At 17 years old, I was in the wrong place at the wrong time. I was dragged through a field and left for dead.

I'm not supposed to be here. Anyone else feel that way? I thought back to my military career over 21 years and when I retired at 40. I remembered the 3 combat tours I'd been through. One of the things the military taught me was endurance.

So as you are going through this, think about what is your battlefield. I had 3 sons and ended up going through a divorce after being married for 18 years. But God blessed me with an encore marriage. Ten years I went through this process. I was focused on my business.

So when Sean came into my life, it was simple. We got married at a mastermind. Why did I share this story? There had to be a point where I made a decision to figure out what my purpose was. Your turning point starts today.

I realize there are four personalities here. First, you are listening to me but it's got to be logical. You are an urchin and you are looking for details and need to make sure everything makes sense.

The second personality is what we call a dolphin, who just wants to have fun. The next is what I call a whale who just wants to serve and help. What happens with a whale going through this process, is you don't know if you want to make an offer, you just want to help and serve. Selling is serving.

The last personality is a shark. A shark is a person that wants to run up to you and they don't need a lot of detail, they just have confidence in you.

How many of you want to walk across the stage in the next 12 months? If you are thinking about which personality you are, write it out.

What I see that happens to many of us, is when I ask how many want to walk across this stage, you need to ask who is leading you now? Russell is here to say he wants to help you. He's one of the most brilliant marketers in the world, and I had no idea. I'd been a part of ClickFunnels but I didn't know this community existed.

So I'm asking, who is leading you?

Would you let a 15 year old lead you? What about a 17 year old? They are too young. This doesn't mean this has to be your story? I got to $28M in 3 years because I used every part of me that had stopped me in the past.

Have you thought about why you are not at the place you want to achieve yet? Why did the people who started along with you exceed you and you are still at a lower place? Have you thought about where you came from? Make the adjustments, it will change your life?

Then something starts to happen. You start getting around people who are warriors. It taught you about resilience, strategy and tactics. The one thing that is missing now is the person who helps you do this. The person you are right now is not the person you will become.

I represent the person who went through all the battles, all the defeat, all the rejection and I made a decision I could no longer allow divorce, depression and bankruptcy lead me. So I decided to let those parts of me from the past go. I thank them and let them go because I know God is calling me for greater things and he allowed things to happen to get me to this point.

With my military past, I'm taking this one with me because it gave me the opportunity to fight and it gave me the strength to understand that a leader leads from the front, not from the rear.

What version of you are you going to keep and what version are you going to release? I do that demonstration to show that someone has to go.

Mindset - many people believe in order to get to a goal, most of this has to be skills and tactics. How many believe it's the mindset to get to a $1M? Many people think you need 20 things to make one thing possible. I know you need one thing to make 20 things possible. That one thing is this community.

Imagine you worked on the version of you who can do the thing. How many of you have a message you want the world to hear? When was the last time you were on social media and went live? When was the last time you told your story? Somebody needs to hear more from you, as a speaker.

Next, write a book. Who will take the challenge to write a book in the next 90 days?

Next thing I recommend is going to events. Imagine having virtual events where you charge each one a $200 ticket. We did that without Facebook ads. I was speaking on stage and I wrote a book.

Create a course. This is what Russell and Tony's been doing over the last 25 years. They speak, they have events, they write books and they do coaching.

Coaching is the simplest thing you'll ever do, you just use your experience and life knowledge. This is something that traditional education will not teach you. Whether you have a degree or not, tap in.

Make an offer - how many get really nervous when you make an offer?

Today is your day. I want to challenge you. For those of you that are not leaving this room the same way you came in, you are looking for leadership and guidance, I'm going to ask you to step out.

I dare you 12 months from now, that you become the person that does the thing. This is so much bigger than money. I represent the future version of you. I'm not smarter, I just took a chance and bet on myself. Will you bet on you?

Russell Brunson

Unlocking the Secrets of the Two Comma Club

We developed this award so people would have something to run towards and drive you. When you have a goal to run towards, it makes it a lot easier.

Step 1 - you have to have a really good offer. A level 10 offer is one where everyone stands up and runs to buy.

Step 2 - create the 1 to many presentations - what are the stories and hooks to present the offer

Step 3 - create the virtual stage

The Real Story Behind The Two Comma Club Award

When John Reese sold $1M worth of product in a day, for me I was no longer okay with making $1,000/month. I knew I have to figure this out. If I was to do that, how could I make $1M in a year? That means making $2,739 each day.

So we started creating a bunch of funnels. It wasn't until I interviewed Vince who sold supplements online and wrote a book about it. I had 6 hours worth of interviews with this guy.

As I was launching ClickFunnels, one day I said I wonder if anyone would buy these interviews I did with Vince. I bought a license from him to sell his physical book. This was the first video upsell ever created.

We launched and on Oct. 16, 2007, this offer was the one that crossed me into the Two Comma Club. I remember I was freaking out but there was no one to talk to about it. I thought that I should get an award for it!

So I decided to create an award for myself. I've won:

- 43 2CC Awards
- 8 2CCX Awards
- 4 2CCC Awards
- 3 Two Heart Awards

- 1 Billion Award

So we created an award for entrepreneurs and the first FHL we had this, there were 73 winners. And people were watching them, thinking they could do it too.

I spent a lot of time reading your comments and I realized the thing holding most people back are what's between your ears. Tony says that tactics are only 10% and the other 90% is the psychology. That's what gets people to win, and that was the first time he spoke at FHL. If you can get your mindset to work, the system is flawless and everything gets easier.

Secret #1 - Your Call To Adventure

How many of you are familiar with hearing the call? It's real and you felt it. It's this call to contribute, do more and be more. You need faith that this call is real and it's helping pull you to become the person you are meant to be. It will be hard, but I promise it will be worth it. If you step into and grasp it, it will change your life forever

Secret #2 - The Story That Protects You Also Imprisons You

Now, I'm going to bring on stage, 7 special guests:

Erik Sorenson

20 years ago, I attended my first seminar. There were guys like Zig Ziglar, Tony Robbins and Stephen Covey. I felt this powerful pull that I should be speaking on stage. And I didn't do anything for 15 years about it. I just went back to my normal life. I started a business and I was so good about figuring out what not to do. For 15 years I kept doing the same thing.

All of a sudden my life started getting worse and worse. I exited that business and I didn't know what to do. I read a quote that changed the course of my life.

"The scariest day of your life is the day you die, when the person you are meets the person you could have become."

I read a book for the first time in 15 years and it was then that I found out about FHL in 2020. I remember listening to these incredible speakers and I saw them win the 2CC award. I heard them say "I was you, sitting in that chair". A few days later, there was an opportunity to join the coaching program.

But all these voices in my head said what if I'm not good enough, so I did nothing. But the calling came again, and I ended up calling my wife. She said she trusted me and I realized that the story that protects you, also imprisons you. The problem with good enough is there is no incentive to rise above.

I went in my room and had an idea for a mastermind. I spent hours figuring it out, and it so happens I was speaking at a small conference in Miami in 2 weeks. I got on that stage and sold 23 people a $25,000 offer. I was halfway to the 2 Comma Club in 90 minutes.

All of these incredible things happened because I finally listened to the right story. The story that scares you, is the one that will save you. Do you believe in yourself and which story do you believe? The version of you in the future that scares you but saves you?

Secret #3 - Getting Your Subconscious Aligned

Your subconscious is driving all of our thoughts and actions. People say they want to change the world but their subconscious says no way can you be successful.

Tyler Watson

How many of you believe that you are holding you back? I'm going to teach you something that will help you confront resistance. If you have something you are struggling with, the trigger is the transformation you have to accept to get to the next level.

One of the things I struggled with was depression, video game addictions, and poverty. It wasn't until I learned how to make a change that lasts. I was trying all the skills but it wasn't working.

U (speed at which you can attain your goals) = Skills (work + focus)

If you are putting 100% effort in but only getting 10% out, it comes down to:

Allergies and addictions in the body

If you have just 10 of these, it robs you.

I'm going to help someone from the audience now. Ariana has a goal of making $10K/month and has been at it for 3 years. When she thinks about it, it brings up anxiety.

I'm holding $10,000 in my hand. Now Ariana is holding the money.
Breathe in and out. Pant like a dog. Smile. In her body, she was having a response toward allergies and addictions.

Now think "I can make this in a month"

Before we did this, now how does it feel? Solid. Change can happen fast, it doesn't have to take years.

Secret #4 - The Big Secret: Turning Pro

You have to step up and become pro.

Eileen Wilder

How many of you want to go fast to get the 2 Comma Club Award? If you don't do this, you will go slow. One of the reasons you have been going slow is you are acting like an amateur. The solution is to act like a pro.

If you bring forth what is within you, what you bring forth will save you. If you do not bring forth that which is within you, what you do not bring forth will destroy you.

1. Decide who you are
2. Get uncomfortable. A lot. Turning pro is free but demands sacrifice. We find our self respect, our power and our voice when we do this.

You must separate to elevate. I read that there are turtles and giraffes. One eats from the tops of trees and one crawls through the grass. You can allow people what they are reporting on their level. You cannot explain to a turtle, a giraffe's decision.

The giraffe has a 25 pound heart to keep his head up. If he lowers his head, he will pass out. Sometimes we lose consciousness because we are hanging out with the turtles.

When you are built to be tall, you will endanger your position if you lower your perspective. Stop looking for approval from people who don't approve of themselves. Stop looking for permission. You have to separate to elevate.

Secret #5 - Creating Your Alter Ego

Bart Miller

Imagine that you have written down all your beliefs on a board and you are standing with that board and you have to break it with your face? This little boy is holding the board and he's so nervous. The instructors can't get him to do it. I looked at him and said "Who's your favorite superhero?" and he said Hulk. I said "Can you be Hulk for a second?" and he punched right through the board.

Then I asked myself, did that little boy get stronger, or smarter in that moment? No, he stepped into a new identity. As entrepreneurs we know what we need to do. But fear, doubt are holding us back. The version of you that got you here is not the version of you that will get you to the next place. You've got to want this.

You can spend thousands of dollars on mindset, imposter syndrome or wait forever. But there's an easy way. It's to step into the identity of a person who already has the result you want.

Russell is an amazing Dad at home and when he wrote DotCom Secrets, he knew he had a calling. So he created Russell Brunson, the man who can sell anything.

You may know Marilyn Monroe but she's also Norma Jean. They asked her how does she go anywhere? She replied she goes as Norma Jean.

Bo Jackson, Beyonce, Kobe Bryant, and Adele all use this superpower.

How do you activate it? Russell uses a watch. Beyonce uses stilettos.

This is how we accelerate. You need to decide who you need to become and activate that to go to the next level.

- Create
- Activate
- Accelerate

Secret #6 - You're the Hero Of The Story

Nadia & Nicole

We worked on Wall Street in investment banks and when we found this world, we decided to create a webinar. It took us 4 weeks to create it. We had a small email list and we were teaching people about financial literacy.

We had about 4,000 people and 200 found out about the webinar. About 50 showed up and we made zero sales. We had some technical difficulties during the webinar but we got data out of it.

When we came to FHL, we said if we're going to do this, we have to be committed. So we decided to follow the framework. The next step in the process was to practice. We found out from the first one there was some confusion. Then we got 3 sales on the next one.

When we did the next two webinars, we didn't sell anything. We realized we needed to change our offer. We looked at the comments and emails, and realized it was not the offer they wanted.

We just finished webinar 15 and we're almost at $50,000.

You have to look at it like a life skill. When you learn to ride a bike or read - it's like a superpower.

Secret #7 - Buy Things With Offers

Myron Golden

The price doesn't matter, if I'm willing to pay the price. How many of you want to get to a point where the price doesn't matter? I'm going to invite someone to come on stage and help me share with you this concept that will change your life.

His name is Byron Silverman. 50% of the production of any domain is produced by the square root of that domain.

If you have 4 salespeople, the square root is 2, so 2 will produce.

If we change the number from 4 to 9, the square root of 9 is 3.
3 of them are going make ½ the commissions
If you have 100 this number is 10
If you have 10,000 the number is 100

This is called Price's Law. (I learned this from Derek J Price)
The bigger the number gets, the smaller the percentage of the producers there are. There are 30 million businesses in the US. The square root is 5,477.

That means the rest have to split the other half.

Almost everybody is willing to do enough to be one of the mediocre but only a handful are willing to pay the price to be one of the fantastic few. The difference between those who win the 2CC award and those who do not is that very few people are willing to pay the price. You are looking at yourself as someone who can't pay the price to become the person that does the thing.

Even fewer people are willing to own the identity. The reason you struggle is you don't know who you are, because you bought into your lie-dentity - all the things and people who told you things that you are not.

You replace your lie-dentity with your my-dentity. But not until you recognize that you are only who God says you are. Your identity comes from the I am.

Every time you say something disempowering after you say I am, what you are doing is you are infusing your limitations with you.

Own the identity of the fantastic few and be willing to pay the price.

Russell Brunson

I have a friend that doesn't have a product, but when you learn this skill set it'll change your life forever. They pitch other people's products and will keep a percentage.

Now, I'm going to answer some questions about Prime Mover.

Question 1 - What is the difference between Prime Mover Foundation & Mastermind?

For either one you only need a deposit for $997.

The PMF is the program that's typically $10K a year. The goal is to:

- Create your level 10 offer
- Create 1 to many presentation
- Create your funnel

These are 6 virtual events that happen. Event #1 you get your offer figured out. Then you transition to module 2 which is a virtual event, and so on. By the time you are done you'll have your offer, presentation and traffic coming into your funnel.

The Prime Mover Mastermind is the program that is $30K a year. You are still getting PMF and we have a quarterly mastermind in Boise. Also, we are doing a mastermind in Mexico. This is where you can congregate in person as well as virtually.

For most people, after you learn the skill set you get your money back.

Question 2 - Do I have to do webinars?

If I'm doing a challenge funnel, all a challenge funnel is a webinar extended over 3-5 days. It also works at live events. One of my friends coaches kids and athletes. He did a one to many presentation to the parents and sold rehab services to them. It also works if you are doing a VSL. You are taking the entire presentation and plugging it in.

So it doesn't matter what you are selling, a one to many presentation is the thing you need. You will notice this stuff becomes second nature when you start speaking.

Question 3 - How much time does it take?

This depends on you and how crazy you are. There are 6 events in the Prime Mover program. Each event focuses on one core thing.

My coaches are on there and there's other people. We teach the principle, you do it and you come back and share it. Throughout the week we have live coaching calls.

These 6 events are happening multiple times each month. Some of you might want to do a module once a week, and some of you might want to get it all done within 2 weeks.

Our goal is to get you your investment back as fast as possible. The goal is to get that $10K back within 1-3 months.

Question 4 - I'm just getting started, can I afford it?

The question is can I afford not to do this? How do we shortcut our success? Money follows speed. Our coaches help pull you through step by step.

Question 5 - When do I have to decide? Right now. After my presentation it will cut off because we will have the welcome celebration.

The worst thing that happens is you go to a big event, you get excited then you return home and nothing happens.

Sometimes I show people what I'm trying to overdeliver with but sometimes people get overwhelmed.

So you have to promise me, if I show you what you get in the coaching program, you won't get overwhelmed. This is the first step but I'm giving you lifetime access.

With the Prime Mover access area, you'll notice 3 things:

- Fountainhead
- Lynchpin
- Alchemy

With Fountainhead, there's 6 modules and when you are finished and have that presentation that's crushing it, the next step is understanding the linchpin.

This is how we dramatically scale businesses. We sold this last year for $25K and you guys will have this for life. It will deal with your continuity, and more. Now you are scaling your business.

The third program is Alchemy, Dan Kennedy's program. You'll have all access to all that as well. You guys will get access to all 3 of these programs for life.

At the first FHL when we introduced the 2 Comma Club award, I did a presentation called You're One Funnel Away.

We had just launched ClickFunnels and I told the story of the last decade of my life, the ups and downs that got us to launching ClickFunnels. It was my hero's journey.

The Evolution

Typically you share your highlight films, but it's not all sunshine and roses. Today I want to talk about the last decade and hopefully you'll understand the hero's journey is not all sunshine and roses.

In 2013, we started building ClickFunnels. Todd was coding things, I was home trying to figure out how to market these things. In 2014, we went to Traffic & Conversion, and Ryan and Perry got on stage, and that year became the year of the funnel. They started talking about it, so we were freaking out.

The weekend after T&C, everyone started talking about funnels and this was insane timing. Todd was great at coding but he's not the best at UI. There was this other guy, who would pop up every now and then asking for projects. I paid him the money to do a project and he'd disappear. He did them all overnight, I wired him money and he's gone again.

We're in the room and I see his name - Dylan Jones on Skype asking me again if I needed help. I told him I needed him to fly to Boise and I would take a week of his time. We get in the room next week and he starts building the UI and makes the most beautiful version of ClickFunnels ever. In a couple of months we had the first version done. We launched it, and there wasn't a really good editor at the time, but the funnel builder was the same.

We were getting closer to our actual launch in September and 2 weeks before the launch, Dylan sent me this video with a drag and drop editor. And I remember watching it 30-40 times and I knew we had to have that editor. So I reached out to him, asking him if needed money again. He was going to launch his editor without a backend. After we went back and forth, we finally figured out a negotiation to make him a partner. Todd and Dylan spent the next 2 weeks to put ClickFunnels and his editor together.

We did a reverse launch where we launched a new feature each day, but it didn't take off. After that, that's when we started different versions. After the 5th time, I went to an event, pitched and it crushed.

Now we're in 2015, and we went back to T&C. I remember Ryan Deiss was on stage and he said because of us, ClickFunnels was built. There was a break out room where I couldn't sell. That's crazy because my name is Russell and sell is literally in my name. One of my friends showed up and I'm on stage. He said imagine if we had a booth with all these gorgeous women and Dave said "how many do you need?"

20 minutes later he said there would be a bunch of gorgeous women funneling into the room. All of a sudden all these people follow the woman into the room. I did my presentation, people were going crazy, and I told them if you want the rest of this presentation I have a DVD at the back. It was crazy, people were freaking out. I remember that night afterwards Dave looked at me and he said he wanted to be part of this.

I told him I couldn't afford him, but we hired him anyway and we brought him at that time.

Next we launched our book. Soon, we started growing like crazy, getting more and more people to sign up.

ClickFunnels was growing so fast, and Todd told me after 10,000 members there might be issues. With the database company we were hosted on, we were their biggest company. I remember speaking at Dan Kennedy's event, I did the pitch, and I was backstage. ClickFunnels was down. A week later, I'm speaking in London and when we landed in London, there were thousands of messages that popped up on my phone. Most of them were very angry because ClickFunnels was down.

I called Todd and he told me that we couldn't get it back up right away…and I didn't know what to do. So they were trying to rebuild it and get this thing back up. I'm in London, we're all jet lagged and I wanted to hide, but I felt like we should do something. I went live and told people that we were down and it's not okay. Instead of me trying to hide, I took ownership and that we were trying to fix it. Everyone started shifting from being angry to understanding.

It was back up 8 hours later on the new servers and we were waiting for a mass exodus. But it didn't increase cancellation and for me it was a good lesson of not trying to hide as a leader. That same year, I could not get any of my friends to use my platform. We decided to start building funnels for people and show them how it works.

We met Neil Strauss, Dave Asprey, Tony Robbins, and Liz Benny. I built funnels for them all, trying to prove this stuff actually works.

I remember Rand Fishkin, the CEO of Moz. I went to one of his events, he's talking about his story, the event ends, and we really wanted to talk to him. He told me "I have a Board of Directors, I live in an apartment, I've been going through depression because I can't grow, because we took on investors, they are making us do things that I'm not comfortable with. If I was you I wouldn't take on any money." It was so cool and such a real moment.

I remember on the drive home, that we decided not to take on any money so we were not being dictated to by a Board of Directors. Everyone of our competitors has taken on money, but we haven't.

In 2016, We decided to get a keynote speaker for FHL and we wanted to get Marcus from The Profit. I'm expecting him to show up in limos, but he jumps out of an Uber and it was so different. We were backstage and he asked me what was happening in the crowd because people were so excited. I explained my story to him and he started asking me how I'd do a funnel for different businesses he owned.

He gets on stage, leaves and messages me later, asking if I wanted to be on The Profit. A month later, he called me live and asked me if I'd be willing to build a funnel for Flex Watches. We're trying to figure out how to build a funnel right on national TV.

A few months later we flew to CA, and it was chaos. It was such a cool thing and it was surreal to see this thing we made up in a basement, that it was being talked about on TV.

The next month I'm at a dinner and was chatting with Dean Graziosi. In the middle of it, I felt another call that I needed to write another book, Expert Secrets. I swore I'd never write another book and I spoke to Dave about it, who got so excited.

Then we started writing Expert Secrets and also decided we should launch a reality TV show. We launched it on TV, building funnels for people. In 2017, Expert Secrets finally gets done and it creates this whole new movement. It was people who didn't know they needed a funnel, they just wanted to share what they knew.

That's when we grew rapidly. In 2017, I remember seeing the Squatty Potty ad, and it had gone viral. I thought this was some of the best copywriting I'd ever seen. I wanted to hire them to make a video for ClickFunnels and they didn't respond. They thought funnels were things people used to scam people. Then, they launched the FiberFix ad, but it wasn't converting. Finally they had to reach out to me asking how to fix it.

They wanted me to build a funnel for them and I wanted them to make an ad for me. So we fixed their funnel. First they hired 3 comedy writers to write a sketch. You go to a cabin in Sundance and see all the scripts and pick your favorite. Then they go back, write a new script and eventually you have the perfect script.

We got to the cabin and you could tell they didn't like us but they felt obligated to help us. We started showing how all these funnels changed people's lives and eventually they got it. So they produced this viral video for us and after that they started using funnels to sell courses.

We were brainstorming how to launch the video as a team, throwing ideas out there. We were trying to get a bunch of influencers to it. We were told we needed to do something crazy like drive a Ferrari off a cliff. Finally, we thought, what if we tried to set a world record. What if we can make the biggest bubble soccer game? In 14 days, Dave rented out the Boise soccer stadium, and we contacted every influencer we knew. I sat for 6-7 hours, making personalized videos for each person.

We ended up setting a world record, and at that event we showed the Harmon Bros. video and it went viral. That gold prospector became the mascot for ClickFunnels.

That same year I got a phone call from someone in my church that was higher up who asked me if I'd ever heard of Operation Railroad? I asked him how I could help, and I got to meet Tim Ballard. We built out this plan on what we would do, mapped out a funnel, and before we were going to present I had a weird feeling that it wasn't the right plan.

I'd met this guy named Nick Nanton earlier and his name popped into my head suddenly. I got this idea that he was going to build this documentary to help this organization. So I reached out to him and told him how God gave me this idea and he agreed. He said if we covered the hard costs they would do it for free.

So Nick ended up making this documentary that captures what happened when they rescued a big group of kids, and fast forward two months later. We were at FHL and 30 days before that I got asked to speak at Grant Cardone's event. I wanted to beat the world record of selling from the stage. We figured it all out, did the presentation and closed $3.2M in sales.

At FHL, this was the first time we introduced the 2 Comma Club Coaching program. We watched the documentary at the event, and it was crazy. During that event, we raised over $1M for Operation Railroad. When we launched the coaching program we made $12M from that. I felt like we were on top of the world.

That same year I went to a mastermind with Dean Graziosi and Brandon Buchard. I told him they should buy the domain Mastermind.com but they said it was too expensive. I found out it was owned by a 2 Comma Club award winner. I reached out, bought it for $600K and gave it to Dean as a gift. After that, we did this insane launch with Dean and Tony and it was great.

In 2019, we got invited back to Grant's event. I did the pitch, my microphone was out, then they gave me a handheld. Then there was a weird echo reverb and no one understands what I'm saying. It was the weirdest thing, and it didn't work.

I also had a chance to go to Fiji with Tony in a mastermind. I told him I loved building funnels and he gave me a great piece of advice. He said why are you trying to be the CEO? I'm not good at the management piece of the business and there was only one person that made sense. That year I stepped down as CEO and gave Dave the reins.

About that time I got this call from a company who was looking to buy us. We started talking to them, and 300-400 buyers were interested in buying. We kept hearing these huge numbers and it was very distracting. This was in 2020 and at the end, there were 4 companies. They started giving us legitimate numbers. Finally, we flew out and we knew the offers would come in the next morning. Both Todd & I would end up with $110M each cash in our pockets. Or there was option 2 to go back, and struggle for a few more years.

I was scared and we kept talking back and forth. I felt there was something we were supposed to be doing. Next thing I know, Dave flew out, we were all sitting in a room trying to figure out what to do.

We were thinking what do we need to do to make ClickFunnels great. It was fun and exciting. We kept talking and decided to push the money away and go change the world one more time. We did this because we love you guys and we know what you are capable of and I don't want to not be part of it.

In 2021, Todd is in building mode, most of our team is going to rebuild this thing. We started doing some acquisitions and we are a week away from closing the Magnetic Marketing offer. A week before, I noticed Dave wasn't feeling too good. He went to the doctor and came back and I see that in the middle of the day, he's praying next to his desk. He told me the doctor told him he has a tumor.

Things started moving so fast, he ended up in surgery, we were all cheering for him. For the next 2-3 months I couldn't sleep and I could only think about his wife, kids and what they were going through. There was so much chaos and pressure, and it was such a scary dark season. I still struggle with sleeping and that year we announced at FHL that we were working on ClickFunnels 2.0.

We thought we were closer than we probably were. Competitors were taking shots at us, and we got closer to the next FHL. It was something we'd been using and we were proud of it. When you build new software, day #1 you don't have a bunch of customers. So we told people it was a beta launch, and in one week we had 16K people join.

But having that many overnight was definitely a Russell mistake. Everyone started to use it and there were a ton of things to figure out. A lot of people didn't like the experience initially and it was tough. People got angry in a really weird way. That year started for me, a really tough time. I started seeing people who were close friends and partners, turning their backs on us.

I remember seeing people who had won a 2 Comma Club award running ads promoting my competitors. I was so frustrated, because there were customers who I gave everything to and they competed against us. I was thinking I didn't want to help people anymore and it was very hard for me.

In 2022, we were working through these issues, and things were improving. In December I was leaving wrestling practice with my kids and I got a message from Dave's wife that I should go by, as it could be the last time I see him. I remember he looked at me and told me I'd changed his life. Shortly after that we had a great memorial for Dave and I still think about how through this whole journey, Dave was always so consistent.

He was always asking me what he could do to help and there was no way I could have gotten myself here without him.

In 2023, that year was tough. I jumped back into the CEO role, and towards the end my twin boys turned 18. We were planning in our minds that they were going to leave, and I don't think we were ready for that. As a parent it gets really scary. We are learning this new phase of parenting and it's emotional and hard.

In 2024, you guys know one of the things I'm so proud of is being present for my kids and I don't think I've missed a wrestling practice my entire career. Once when I was working with the Harmon Bros, I chartered a plane for $30K so I wouldn't miss their wrestling meet.

There was a tournament, and my son was wrestling, and what I did was completely wrong. I pushed the kid off of him as he was doing an illegal move to my son. After that I apologized to the family. Of course, someone caught it on video and it went viral. People I thought were friends started posting the video. I even made it on the Joe Rogan show and I got probably between 3,000-4,000 death threats.

That was hard. I want to serve people but I don't want people to turn on me. How do I show up? I don't feel worthy now. I remember seeing Andy Elliott online and I messaged him. He told me to come out to Arizona, I got to his place and the Elliott army started shaking the jeep I arrived in. He says this is the way you introduce Russell Brunson. Then all these guys stripped off their clothes and they started wrestling. I saw drones flying above, they wanted me to wrestle too and I agreed.

I was thinking I don't know who these kids are, but I can't say no. We were wrestling on this mat, but the scorching sun made the mats get so hot. So they pulled the mat to the shade and we're onto match #2, and I beat him. Eventually I was done and for the next 10 hours, Andy kept telling me "Do you know who you are? You are Russell Brunson and you changed my life!"

He reminded me who I was and it felt good. I started thinking about the last two decades. It didn't matter what the people I helped did with that, it mattered how I helped them. There will always be headaches and it just happened. That's okay, it doesn't prevent you from going forward with your mission. It doesn't matter who you are. People are going to come after you.

I'm still in the game with the rest of you, in the trenches every day. I'm still a funnel hacker every day. Even if people are laughing at me, I've been called to do something greater. As I remember who I am, it's my job to get you to remember who you are. I know where I'm going and I'm stepping into a new hero's journey. It's not the end, it's the beginning.

This last decade has also been more fulfilling, seeing what you guys have done with this stuff. 20 years ago, no one cared about sales funnels, but our job right now with OfferLab is uniting the community. All that matters is the mission. I'm here to serve you guys because I believe in you. I also know how hard that call is and I can't do it on my own.

Gary Halbert - "*Properly exploited, one good idea that occurs to you while walking on a beach his worth more than 10 lifetimes of hard work*"

One thing Dave would always tell me is this is not just the business, this is something from God and we can't stop. The reason why we didn't take that $110M is because I know the impact and ripple effect that will happen when you guys take your message out to the marketplace.

Russell Brunson
The Last Dance - What's Next....

I have some ideas and plans and they are all really exciting. I know where I'm going and I have some clarity on that. The path has some fog and smoke, but I know where I'm headed.

When we launched all you guys started meeting up on your own. I wanted to meet up with you people, so the first year we had about 600 people show up. It was right after I launched my book, and I had won a Ferrari in an affiliate contest. I was going to give it away to whoever sold the most amount of my books as an affiliate. We had the car on the side of the stage and we also launched the dream car contest.

So we also brought in a corvette to showcase that.

We decided next year to do round two in San Diego, where we had our first paid speakers. Then in year three, we went to Dallas and for me, this mission became tangible. We introduced the 2 Comma Club award and it gave people something to attain. That's when things took off.

In 2018, we were in Orlando. This is when we launched the 2CCX coaching program and from there we went to Nashville. People started making more money, and we went back in 2020. After that we went back to Orlando, which was right before the covid lockdowns happened.

Todd knew about covid before it happened and he made us all use hand sanitizer. A week later we all got home and the whole world shut down. Those who experienced FHL 2021 gave us a solid presentation to handle what came afterwards.

After that in 2022, no events happened. Finally we set another date and I was scared thinking what if people didn't show up. Traffic & Conversion Summit was the week before, they had sold 3,000 seats and we had to. Hardly anyone showed up to that event and I started to freak out.

I had to spend $1M on food and beverage, plus there's a room block. If you guys don't stay here, we have to pay for the rooms. I had a friend that went bankrupt from that. But that didn't happen, and it was crazy. You guys showed up and at that event, Tony spoke. He had a 3 hour block, and at the end he asked me if he could go longer. I think he talked for 6-7 hours that day.

He went off on a little rant about vaccines, someone filmed it and the next day we made it onto TMZ. In 2023, we went back to Orlando, and after that we decided we wanted to do FHL International 6 months ago so we could bring it live, back to this time of year.

Then, the next question is why is this the last one? I remember growing up I went to Armand Morin's seminar, then he ended The Big Seminar. There's a couple reasons why. First, I'm tired. This is my 11th presentation in the last 4 days. It's a lot of work for me and my team. It's a 10 month+ process to get people in the room. The cost to run this gets bigger and bigger each year.

I think this year it's over $6M, not counting the ads we run to get you to come. You know we also have a software and coaching business. For me, I need a little break.

Will I ever bring it back? I don't know the answer. It was interesting, and there's so much value having an industry event. I have a vision for something that looks something like this but different. Over the last decade, other events are looking more like this. I need more space to create what it is. We can grow bigger and I want to make something that you won't expect. But I need a couple of years to figure out what that is.

This year, I took two of my kids to where Mike Tyson fought Jake Paul. About halfway through the event, we were talking about the fight in Madison Square Garden with John Jones. Earlier that day, we were in Dallas and I told my kids we had to see where JFK was shot. I'm a little bit of a conspiracy theorist, so we went down there. The first half of the experience you go up into the repository and they have their version of the story with the lone gunman.

Then you go down to the grassy knoll where there's the six books that talk about the conspiracies. I bought all the books and we were having so much fun. Then we are getting closer to the Tyson fight and we were thinking about still going to New York. I asked Siri what airport is closest to Madison Square Garden and it's JFK. It's a sign! So I booked the trip, we flew to New York, watched the fight and we were right next to where all the fighters walked out. It was such an insane experience.

Prince Ea told me he opened for U2 and all of a sudden I imagined this vision - can you imagine if FHL was held at Madison Square Garden someday?

What about the 2CC Awards?

We are going to be introducing a new event, where people have a chance to get their awards. We'll do the awards ceremony there, and during the event each of the winners will have a chance to give a talk, walking you through what they did. These will be like little Ted Talks. I wish every winner can tell their story and the vision I have of this is going to be very cool.

What about the community?

The biggest downside is we do it once a year and we go back home. I started thinking back to how ClickFunnels started. We tested this a lot the last few months, holding ClickFunnels Connect events. These are small meetups and the first few we've had had been a huge success. At these events we have our developers and a bunch of people.

It's kind of like a meetup and each one of you will have the opportunity to create a meetup group and you can do little versions of FHL together. We want to make a coordinated one once a month. We'll bring in either a 2CC winner, me or someone else who will stream directly to you.

Another thing we want to do is, like on the Bachelor. Every week people throw these bachelor parties in the house and Chris Harrison would randomly show up. My vision is after we start doing this, after you register for an event, either I or Todd randomly shows up. So this conversation doesn't have to end.

Those of you who decide to run things, will have special things available for you.

What about legacy? This is not just about my legacy but what about yours? Some of you know that over the last few years I've been collecting a bunch of books and creating a building. While I'm building this, I'm thinking about how to create an offer that will help fund this. What if I made an offer where they can donate $1M to be a part of this legacy.

I went to Mexico but I got scared to pitch it. Eileen Wilder leaned over and convinced me to do the pitch. She helped me write out the offer, and I ran out on stage. I'm freaking out and I had so much fear. I showed the vision of what I was trying to create and then I made the $1M offer with a video.

I wanted to offer a seat license. For example, if Tony Robbins is coming for an event, you'd get first right of refusal to purchase that show, and if you did not want it, it would go to the open market. I wanted to make this offer completely irresistible, so every licence someone has covers a virtual seat license. You can tell your community you are going to hear Michael Jordan for 3 days and you've got 30 tickets to sell. You sell those 30 tickets for $3K a piece, which is a huge benefit.

It gets your highest level mastermind members to stick around longer and you can get your investment back. For those of you in the front row, you also have a chance to hold your own event here, teaching live. That alone will cover the investment of the event. At the end, your teachings will be part of the event center forever. My goal is to extend you and your legacy forever.

In 100 years from now, I don't want your legacy to end. If we don't figure out ways to extend your legacy, it'll be gone forever.

We made two offers - a million dollar seat plus a $100K seat license. We did that for a small group. We raised $14M from that one offer.

Who do you think was the first person that ran and bought this thing? Myron Golden

Myron - Why was I the first to buy this seat? I was thinking about Russell and his journey and how far he's come. I was thinking about Jeff Bezos and when he started Amazon, it didn't make any products. There are people who thought Jeff lost his mind when he said he was going to sell books out of his garage. I could see the trajectory of Russell's life, and I knew when that train got to the station I wanted to be on.

I wanted to be the first person to say yes to this million dollar offer because I understand that you don't get what you want in life, you get what you are. A lot of you want the big numbers but you are not that kind of buyer, so you don't know the feelings when you make a million dollar offer.

When I realized it was a self liquidating offer, the first event I do, I will 10X my investment. You are not investing in Russell, you are investing in yourself through Russell's dream. That's why I bought it.

How do you make a million dollars seem free?

Inside the $1M offer, there's 2 seats.

To be able to run an event, you get to keep all that money. We also added $100K seat licenses. It should never be a cost, it should be an investment.

We are about a year away from completion of the building and I'm going to be running small events from there. We've also added this cool room, which will be small and intimate.

Then you have the event center with the first two rows being $1M seats, the next 3 rows are $100K seats, then we have some $50K seats.

The $1M seats include running a live event where I will work with you personally and our team will produce it. I want you to make it the perfect event. You'll also get 50 seat licenses for virtual events.

$100K - you get 2 seats at the second tier and can come to the live events.

$50K - you get 1 seat

How many want to come to the grand opening? If you signed up for Prime Mover, you can come for free.

Tony Robbins

It's a privilege to be back here and I've understood thousands of you have done something that many businesses never do. That is to break $1M in revenue. Now you can set the next goal because it's not about the number. If you are going to get to 5, 10, 100 or a billion or more, it requires more strategy and maximizing you to a different level.

Have you gone back to your home town and see that people still go to the same burger place after all these years? But there's a place called McDonalds which sucks but they understood the business. You have to understand how to run a business.

This is my 48th year of doing this. In that time, I've learned so many distinctions and some of them have helped me to build companies. I own 85 private equity firms along with my businesses and if you combine them that's half a trillion dollars of business.

I started with absolutely nothing, but early in my life I was obsessed and that's what makes a difference in people's lives. Why do some people give them everything and still end up in rehab? There's others who start with nothing and become like Oprah.

I had 4 different fathers at one point and I wasn't popular but I always loved people. It made me understand what influences people the most. As I dug in, it doesn't matter where you come from I realized. There really is no limit to your creativity and hard work.

I remember early in my career I went to work for Jim Rohn and I asked him why all my fathers are broke. On Thanksgiving when I was 11, my parents were saying things to each other that once you say you can't take them back. There was a knock at the door and there was this giant guy with a frozen turkey. He asked for my dad and I ran to get him. Inside I was so excited, and my dad opened the door. But when he saw the guy, he went to slam the door and didn't want to take the turkey. But the guy said I'm just the delivery guy.

The man was not mean and saw me in the background. He said "please don't let your family suffer because of your ego". My dad's shoulders dropped, he took the groceries, didn't say thank you and put them on the table. I was shocked. That event is why I'm here today.

Shortly after that, my father left the family and I didn't understand. I believe decisions control our lives. Everyone can have tough things but it's your decision on what you focus on.

What are you going to focus on? Your life, joy, and business is all controlled by what you focus on. What's wrong is always available and so is what's right. Have you read something a friend did and you say you can't believe it? Then you confront them and find out its total bullshit. Our focus controls the way we feel. Most of us allow our phone or the tv to control our focus.

You can focus on your hair, or a million other things. Our brain is generalizing so we don't have to think too much. The minute we focus on something here's the 2nd decision we have to make:

What does this mean? Our brain is looking for anything that can harm you. But we react to what people say about us. Is this the end or the beginning? If you think it's the end of the relationship are you going to behave like it's the beginning? If you are that in love with something, what will you do? But after 7 days, 7 weeks, 7 years, will you still do anything? When you give a new meaning to your relationship you behave differently.

Is this person challenging me? Is this person loving me? Are they dissing me? We get to decide the meaning but we don't do it consciously.

Meaning = emotion and emotion = life.

If you are angry you'll have a different response than if it's playful or love.

My dad's focus was that he did not take care of his family. I had a different set of focus. There was one meaning I chose - which was that strangers care. Up until that point I thought we lived in a wealthy community and we were treated that way. But someone who delivered food to us, shifted my whole life. So I decided I'm going to do this for at least two other families.

I learned some skills, and I worked for Jim Rohn. I remember asking him how come my dads were always broke? Jim told me we are all equal at souls but we are not all equal in the marketplace. You have to understand your business. He said if someone works at McDs and complains about minimum wage, they don't understand the system. If you work there, that's supposed to be your first job. That job doesn't get paid much.

No risk, no reward. They want guarantees just by sticking around. You have to take risks, and add value. The guy who made a billion dollars made $40M for his clients. So he's worth it. Find a way to add more value than anyone else in the marketplace and you will dominate. That means do more for others than anyone else.
I see people in relationships that ended and the most common thing I hear is "I gave them everything". But I say everything except what they wanted. Or they wouldn't have left.

If you want a million clients, fall in love with your clients, not your service.

There was also added value outside your business. When I was 17, I went to this grocery store and said I was going to buy food for two families. Then I thought I didn't want them to react like my dad did, so I wrote a note that it was a gift from a friend, please enjoy it and someday if you can, do it for a family as well.

So I borrowed my friend's van, drove to a house, knocked on a door, and the woman screamed when she saw me. I said I was only the delivery boy, and she took the food and said "Gift from God". It was amazing. It was a tiny place and I heard these screams and 4 boys came in to watch me. There was that belief.

So I gave her a hug and I'm looking in my rearview mirror and these tiny kids are on her porch. By the way, her husband had left her 4 days before. I realized that was my best day. If my father had not left, I didn't think I'd be there that day. I kept doubling the donations and eventually got to 4 million donations a year. Most people overestimate what they can do in a year and underestimate what they can do in a decade.

Time goes by so fast and it feels faster as you get older. Some of you will not realize how valuable what you are doing now is. I was writing a book about 10 years ago and while I was writing, Congress had cut food stamps from 6 billion dollars. So I called my office and they said I'd fed 42 million people.

I want to see if you can pick up a moonshot for yourself. What would that be like? If the size of your goals affect you, you'll come up with a plan. What if I did more? What if I did 100 million for 10 straight years - a billion years. And I did it in less than 8 years.

There's about 11 countries on the verge of famine and we need fertilizer. So I created another meal challenge with a partnership from a gentleman from the UN. And we've done 30 billion meals. I tell you that as a metaphor for your business.

80% of the success of your business is psychology and 20% is strategy. There are people who have the same strategy who are doing $10M and those who are doing nothing. It's your emotional energy because if you are just doing something for you, you won't get far.

If you are in a situation, life gives you ideas on how to do it. I married a woman when I was 25 who had 2 kids and that made me grow. If you are trying to serve a community, find something that you care about more than yourself, like Russell. That is why he has so much power. That process will give you the energy to follow through when things don't quite work out.

I want you to think about what it will take to go through the next level. So I thought what we would do is give you a few distinctions and make you think. If you are going to grow, all you have to realize is that the whole game of life is based on patterns. You don't get angry each moment or get lonely. You get sad when certain things don't work out. You have patterns and people think they are their patterns. But you are not, you have a mind and a soul.

I got obsessed about the patterns that make you feel joyous and passionate, and if you understand how to trigger those you can instantly trigger your performance. We are living in a time when you have to know these patterns. Between AI and robotics, in the next 5 years there will be more change in the human race than in history and most people are not prepared for it. I work with some of the best financial people in the world and I've seen their offices go from a few hundred down to 20.

About 45% of all jobs are going to go away. Now they will be replaced by new jobs but you'll have to learn quickly.

How long will it take before all vehicles are automated? It's less than 5 years. Who is going to hire a truck driver that only drives 8 hours a day and wants healthcare? 5 million jobs are going away. That's one category.

You should know that's happening. But the biggest problems are the biggest opportunities.

150 years ago 95% of Americans were farmers. Now it's 3% that feeds the whole world.

You need to arm yourself and when I look at my kids and grandkids I want to see how I can arm them. You need to learn 3 skills.

The first skill to master is pattern recognition. When you recognize patterns you will no longer be fearful.

People will say we've never been as divided as a country, but if you think that, you are completely wrong. Look at the Adams vs. Jefferson ticket. They said absolutely horrible things against each other. These are our founding fathers.

When you understand patterns, you no longer think it's chaos. Losers react - winners anticipate. How many have played a video game with a child? You think you'll be fine and you're dead in two seconds. Now the child starts and 45 minutes later you get your second turn. They win because they've played this game before.

You can do the right thing at the wrong time and you get nothing.

The second skill is Pattern Utilization - if you know anyone that's done well with anything, understands how to use patterns. Speilberg knows how to move the camera, when to bring the camera up, etc. Business is a pattern and when you know these you'll have an advantage over everyone else.

The third skill is Pattern Creator - in the beginning when you play the piano, most of us play other people's music. But after a while, you know the patterns and think you can make my own music. That's the goal you want to achieve.

We live as fearful creatures, most of our time as humans. Mostly we lived as hunter gatherers. When we recognized the patterns of seasons, we learned if you planted in a season other than spring, you are screwed. But if you plant at the right time, you always get rewarded.

When we learned that pattern it changed all of humanity. We have seasons in our life. In springtime, it's easier for things to grow. We can look at our lives as seasons. 0-21 is easy and in that stage life is mostly about supporting you. You are going to be protected. You are learning, growing and you get to that point at 21, when you think you know everything.

Summertime is ages 21-41 - this is the most unhappy time for most people. This is when you test what you are learning. What happens is, you are in the soldier society. If there's a war, you are going. That's also when you figure out a relationship at this station. If you run a business, you have to make it grow. You are being tested and you are trying to prove yourself.

Fall is ages 42 - 62 - midlife, the power season. This is the season where if you did your job, you are reaping on a massive scale. If you are in that season, that is mind boggling because the growth really comes through. You know the people, the relationships and you make things happen.

Winter is 62 -> that's the elderhood. It's the happiest time of your life, if you take care of your health. Because you have long relationships, you know who you are and you are not trying to prove yourself to anyone. You have lots to give and you want to give.

Every season has opportunities and challenges. In the season I'm in, I have friends that are dying. In summertime, you're still figuring it out.

The last thing is there are seasons in history. Let's pretend you were born in 1910 and when you hit 21, it was the roaring 20s. Then all this new technology came out. We have radios, cars. Television and the economy exploded in the fall. So those kids were thinking I'm going to party and they were looked down upon by others. They were called flappers and had never seen anything rough. But when they turned older, we had the depression in 1929, people were standing in line for bread.

That generation that was so weak - how do you get muscle? You have to lift the heavy weights. These people went through 10 years of depression. They made it through from 1929-39 and now they are about to turn 30. Finally the depression is over and WW2 starts. The stock market crashes and the weakest people became the strongest. They call them the greatest generation. They went through D-Day, and fought for us.

They came back and created a baby boom. If you were a veteran we gave you a house, and we created urban America. If you think about the late 40s and 50s, the general population's mood was optimism. After you make it through winter, you go through spring.

No winter lasts forever, they are always followed by a beautiful spring. Did you ever smile so much your face hurt? Every 10-15 years, the mood changes. America was happy until the 70s, then the Vietnam war came. Now there's a conflict through the generations. Think about the 60s and 70s.

The X generation is a small, powerful group and changed their views. They created grunge, dressing casually, and the world changed. Then we had the 1980s-2000s where people were more economically driven.

Now, spring is in sight. We need to make changes where there is more freedom and choices. We now have a place but we are not there yet. There will be more economical challenges and there will probably be a war. But on the other side there will be 15-20 years of optimism.

Your psychology is controlled by the level of energy they bring to the table. Today because of Covid, the average person spent 4 years sitting and that's what they are used to. Companies are telling their people they need to come back to the office. They wonder why they are not happy. We are entering a new season and it starts with the energy. You have to be aware that the energy around you is so low. The whole world has adjusted.

I read that the average person gained 16 pounds during covid. So if you are not going to transform, we need to create energy. If you get up and don't want to talk to people, and fake it, people will sense it. If there's a big problem, who do you want on your side? Someone who knows what to do and says "Move, I'll take over."

Have you seen a singer that was ugly, but when they sing it's amazing?

What if you have two people who are in love with each other and they have high energy but they let life wear them down a bit. Now their energy is just ok. It's not going to be the same relationship. What if they allow themselves to get exhausted and are in a lousy state? The ability to change your state/your energy level is the most important thing in life.

Where does energy come from? It comes from psychology and it also comes from movement. The word competition comes from the Latin word to conspire together. When we compete, you push me as hard as you can to make me better. We are going to compete for energy.

If we are going to take whatever season we are in and maximize it, what makes you a leader is the standard you have for yourself. I want you to notice how to influence people, but what makes you a leader is how you can influence thoughts, feelings of another human being.

To influence another human being you have to know what already influences them. How many have more than 1 child? I'm sure you don't have a favorite child but how many have an easier one? And I bet that the easier one is more like you.

There's 2 things that influence anyone:

1. Emotional state moment to moment.
2. Blueprint - long term. This is their belief system, their values.

Of the two, the one that is most powerful is the state because if you change your state you can change your blueprint.

If you put your hands together, you'll notice you have the same thumb on top. If changing thumbs makes you uncomfortable, imagine how uncomfortable changing your life will be.

If your left thumb is on top of your right thumb, the driving psychology is sex and amazing lover. If your right thumb is on top then the driving force is intelligence and you'll be financially free in your lifetime.

I want you to turn to your neighbor and greet people as if it wasn't important. How many people were quiet and had no energy? If you understand the triggers in your body, you'll do something else. This time I want you to greet people as if they would reject you. Let's have someone come on the stage as an example. I'm afraid of her, I'm going to exaggerate that if I'm like a little kid.

I want you to exaggerate your fear and go up to people as if you are deathly afraid of them. Did you use your body in the same way? Did you breathe more shallowly? Did you talk louder or quieter? Did you talk faster or slower? What was your voice like? Notice that is your fearful state.

Let's try a different one. I want you to greet someone, where if they don't like you immediately then your kids won't eat and everyone you care about will die.

Did you use your body differently? Did you use more of the muscles in your face or less? Did you talk louder or quieter? Did you touch them? Did it feel good? Why? Because emotion is created by motion. If you use more of the gifts your creator gave you, then you will feel more of those gifts. But most live in a box.

You need to break out of the box and move.

Now, I want you to greet someone as if they are your long lost lover or friend. How did you greet them? It's also sound, and the deepest part of our brain is affected by that.

How many of you like to sing when no one is around? And when we don't sound good? It feels good and your job is to transfer your emotion. People don't buy based on logic.

How many have seen people in parts of the country where a tornado came through and everything got wiped out? How many think to themselves, why don't they move? They consider it a home and we have an emotional home. How many of you know someone that's not really funny but they think they are?

What do you want from your business? Do you want impact? But that's a feeling. Someone else - to change lives. Why do you want to change lives? If I change lives, my life will change. How do you know? It's the way you feel.

So when people tell me they want money, what you really want is freedom, security, and contributions - they are all feelings.

You don't want a relationship, you want love or a connection or partnerships. You wanted a feeling.

All it takes is to be able to change what your emotional home is. I want you to write on a page, on the left side, the emotions you experience at least once a week that are positive. Then on the right side, write down the negative emotions you experience at least once a week. I'm looking for the patterns because this is controlling your life, your business, your happiness.

How many have 100 emotions? 100
How many people have 75 emotions? 5
How many have 50?
How many have basically 12 emotions? Most people

You can feel over 4,000 emotions, so how many of you think you're getting a little ripped off? Circle the most powerful emotion on your list. Look at the positive two and the negative two. If you take one or two positive emotions that are so positive that they push you through the negative one, what would they be? Love? Laughter? Passion? Faith? Curiosity? If you made those two emotions primary in your life, how would that make your life better?

If you want to get a targeted result, whatever the target is, that will only be hit by new action. But you are only going to do that if you are in a different state than before. Most people work on the action, but that's a mistake.

For example, "I know, I need to go on a diet, so I'm going to work out and eat better". But if they say that with low energy they won't do it.

What's easier: dieting or fasting? Fasting because there's no negotiation and it's easier to do. When most people are dieting they are trying. So all of us need to ask ourselves "If I want this behavior what state do I need to naturally do that behavior?"

I remember I was in Japan and I got in this elevator, these 2 women looked up at me, and I said to them "You're probably wondering why I called this meeting". They laughed because I was in a playful state.

The fastest way to change your state is your physiology.

You already experienced changing your state. Jump and down and create a sense of excitement. You can change your state in a heartbeat.

When we do a fire walk, it's taking people through an experience they think is impossible. If you put your shoulders back, and say yes, then they can do it.

The second way to change your state is to change your focus. Our focus controls what we feel as well. I remember working with Andre Agassi, the first athlete I worked with. He went from #1 to #19 in 9 weeks and he was very frustrated. He was dating Brooke Shields at the time, and he said he didn't need positive thinking but she convinced him to come to my house.

So he sits down and says "do your thing". I said let's start with the attitude. I asked him to tell me what's going on, and he talked about his wrist, and his frustrations. I said to close your eyes, remember a moment when you hit the tennis ball perfectly.

I said when you did that, were you ever focused on your wrist? He said no. I said all we have to do is put you in the state where you performed your best. I rolled out my TV and showed him a video of when he won at Wimbledon and how he walked out.

He walked out and hit his pony tail and said it just felt good. He was thinking why did the other person even show up. I put on a tape during the open when he lost. He walked out in a much different way. He said I was looking at that guy thinking about how he'd beat me. He started to win after that, and gave me all the credit.

When a woman buys a Louis Vitton purse, she doesn't buy it because it's durable. How much did you pay? About $3,500. How much do you think it costs to make? About $20.

If you think you are a practical person, you buy a practical purse. If you think you are the best, you buy the best.

How do you change your focus? You ask questions.

What's something you are proud of right now? How many of you have done some things that were really hard and you are proud of it? Now how do you breathe when you are feeling proud? What is the look on your face when you are feeling proud? Breathe like you do when you are feeling proud. Remember that thing. How many can feel differently in your body.

Now, think of something in your life that you are grateful for? How do you feel when you are grateful? What's the look on your face when you feel grateful? What is the look on your face when you feel grateful?

Think about a loving moment with your family or friends. How do you breathe when you think of that? What's the look on your face? Notice you move differently.

Think of a sexy or romantic moment in your life. How are you breathing now? How many of you can feel that way now? If you really want something exciting now, how many of you can focus on something that's exciting in your life? How do you breathe when you are excited? How do you sound, move, when you are excited?

This is how history is shaped. I'm a big student of history and years ago I got a call from George Bush, Sr. He told me he wanted to invite me to something. They were bringing together leaders from all over the world. He said he heard I was going to be in NY and was wondering if I could bring Gorbachev on my jet. At that time, I was chartering jets, I didn't own one.

I said, do you mind asking Mr. Gorbachev to make a video for some kids I was mentoring and he said yes. So I got to NY, he arrived and we got on the plane. I said we were going to do this interview but he had a bad headache and couldn't do it. We got on the plane and he closed his eyes immediately.

So I had one burning question and I figured I'd talked to his wife and get her to say something that was contradictory. He came around and I asked him "I wanted to know what ended the cold war". He turned and gave me a basic answer: eventually we resolved our issues with Reagan. I said I wanted to know the exact moment it ended.

He thought for a while and said that's a good question.

Then he started laughing this silly laugh and said "I will tell you the moment. Mr. Reagan was sitting across the table and I said you are not here to lecture me, I was burning red and Reagan stood up said this is not working, walked 3 steps and said "can we start fresh?". You had to love the guy and I thought this is a guy I can do business with."

Our entire world changed because someone changed their state. So if it works for changing human history, maybe it will work for sales.

Exercise

1. Write down why you came here?
2. What business are you in and how's business?
3. What's the chokehold on the growth of your business?

Who has something they want to share?

Speaking and leadership, and my business is average. The chokehold is the ability to sell like you and I think I'm a good teacher but I can't change the emotions of people.

How many of you want to speak just to have influence? You might be starting out with the right content. I'm not a great speaker, but I know how to influence people. Are you focused on the wrong subject matter?

Maybe I don't have enough stories and there's too much focus on content.

How do you currently market your business? *Webinars and ads*
Why should I buy from you? *Because I have a great model of leadership that no one else has.*

Maybe that's because it doesn't work. This is where you have to call it tight with yourself. Because sometimes it's appropriate to not just feel good with yourself. I feel you are sincere and authentic, but I feel you can't articulate enough of your ideas to want to do business with you. You have to learn how to speak but it won't make your business grow. You need to build a brand. You understand the power of branding.

Let's do another exercise:

- Write down the name of a large computer company
- Write down the name of a soft drink
- Write down a search engine

How many people wrote down Apple for the first question? Does Apple have the energy? The difference is state. Apple has the energy and a 3 trillion dollar state difference. They created raving fans and when Steve came back he decided his brand was not computers.

He took $1 and some stock and answered how to change the brand. He came up with this little computer in different colors. His biggest change was he thought about what business he's really in. Microsoft was controlling 94% of the computer business at the time.

Steve finally came up with their essence. We make things simple and beautiful and connect people to their passions. And that changed the company. Now Apple is a phone company.

If you have to pause when someone asks you why someone should buy, you need to address that.

If I said think of a search engine, how many thought of Google? Pretty much everyone. How many thought of Bing? Only 2 people.

I could show up anywhere and people know me, because I built a brand. For decades I delivered more value over the years.

Pepsi challenged Coke years ago with the Pepsi challenge. Then Coke came around and said they were going back to the old formula with "New Coke". Then it took them 18 years to make a profit with new coke because they didn't understand their brand. You need to start articulating your competitive advantage.

5 Steps to Creating a Unique Identity

1. Understand the true power of identity. Nothing builds a brand more than your ownership of the value you add
2. Identify and articulate your competitive advantage
3. Practice communicating concurrently - if you have to think about it, it kills the energy
4. You need to live it
5. You need to market it - the most powerful way is to give people experiences of what you do

Tell me did you come up with a better way of describing yourself? *Yes, I study charismatic leaders like Tony Robbins and I can teach how to be a more charismatic leader in your business.*

Be careful of using other people though, what if they don't like the people you use? But I think that was a big improvement.

If you are brand new, you can do it for free for a few people, but the most powerful thing is to do more for someone than anyone else.

I had a friend named Mike years ago, and he wanted to be a realtor but he didn't have a car yet. So he got paid to deliver magazines to people's houses, then when he turned 18 he could get a real estate license. He worked for 18 months and didn't get one listing. He told me no one was trusting him and I said you need to do something for your community. Just keep doing things as someone that cares for the community.

A few weeks later, he said in his area, it's high end, but the trash didn't get picked up for 3 weeks and it started to smell. I thought, "What if I paid a private junk haul service in my part of the community?" I told him he shouldn't pay and instead, you take it all away and don't tell anyone you did it. So he did it.

Imagine you live in a wealthy community and it smells and sure enough all the trash is gone. But the trash strike is still going on. The whole community is trying to figure it out and it got out that Mike had done it. They wanted to pay him, and I told him not to take their money. He didn't but said if you ever know someone that wants to sell, think of me. In the next two years he made $1.2M in selling homes.

You don't need a lot of money to do this. You can harness social media.

For example, here's a product no one would have been interested in. The CWS vacuum cleaner.

Then there's Mike from The Dollar Shave Club. He felt all these companies charged too much for razors. He came up with his ad for $4,500. He sold that company to Gillette 6 years later for $6B. His value was humor. You have to remember what people want.

Here is another interesting example - The haunted house ad - they made this for $45K.

In 1999, the whole world was going to end because of Y2K. Imagine if someone got you to invest in a company and they were going to sell women's shoes? You'd hesitate because people want to try them on.

Every company I've taken over, there are certain fundamentals. Here's 3 ways to grow any business:

1. Who is your ideal client? Who is going to buy multiple things, tell everyone about you, lead others to buy from you, who might influence people? Be specific about what is their pain? What do they hate? Who is going to love this product? What are their pains, problems and what excites them? You have to know what makes them tick.
2. What is your irresistible offer?
3. Over deliver and add more value than expected

Women buy 15 times more shoes than men. So you have the ideal client, but what is your irresistible offer? Without one you don't have a company, you have a job. Something people think it's so good they'd be crazy not to buy.

With the shoes there was too much friction of sending shoes back. Instead, we should say we'll pay the shipping to and from. But women will take a shoe they like and keep it for the future when it fits.

Every company that I have, I find out who is our ideal client. People live between what you desire most and what you fear most. I'll do more than anyone else and then I'll have raving fans.

That's how Domino's Pizza transformed. It was purchased by this guy and it wasn't doing well. He thought, what if I shut this down and we just deliver? His location was ideal because he was close to a college. His sales went berserk. Then he expanded but he didn't realize what made him successful.

He moved to another place away from colleges and his pizza showed up cold. One customer called up so angry, and he said here's what I'm going to do. I'm going to send another one and if it doesn't arrive there within 30 minutes it's free.

He took that experience and that became their irresistible offer. "30 minutes or less or it's free".

Subaru in the 90s was going bankrupt. So they hired a consultant who would figure out who owns one already and sell to those people. It was lesbians. No one advertised to lesbians in those days and they did the first ad with lesbians in them and they had a 3,000% increase.

If you remember Columbia House Records, they built a billion dollar company on that offer of getting 6 CDs for a dollar.

If you do these 3 things, you are going to dominate.

I want you to notice something. I interviewed people to feel what they were feeling and people say things like they lost family members, or they are overwhelmed, or they have imposter syndrome. We are all dealing with the hero's journey. You are living your life, and something that looks like it's the worst thing that could ever happen. But looking back you are thankful for it, because it made you stronger. The secret is to keep that state.

There's a process called stacking. Have you ever overreacted to something? The reason you do that is you are emotionally stacked. You are reacting that it happened again. So in life it's very easy where the news people have one job - to startle you. Their job is to make more money for their shareholders and they need to capture your attention.

When we are constantly being bombarded by things, and we shut off. Your brain is not designed to make you happy, it's designed to make you survive.

So what I do is called emotional stacking. It means you have to stack the good things. I want you to take a deep breath, exhale and moan. Your brain and heart are electrical. When you experience gratitude, the brain and heart are in unison, and that's where you get answers.

If you have some unfinished business that you keep putting off, I want you to think about how stressed you'd be if you focused on that. Now that you know what it is, take your hand and put it on your heart. Feel like you are breathing deeply into your heart with strength. Feel the strength and beauty of your heart. What are you proud of that your heart feels in this lifetime? As you touch your heart, pour gratitude into it.

Pour some love in your heart for the gift of life it gives you. Focus on 3 moments in your life that you can feel super grateful for. Feel the moment. Gratitude destroys two emotions - fear and anger. You can't be grateful and angry simultaneously.

Some of you have heard of HeartMath. They discovered the heart affects the brain and vice versa.

Reach out with your hand and grab a loving moment in your life that you are proud of. Now do it again and grab a romantic moment from your life. Enjoy it. Reach out and get another romantic or sexy moment and say yes - see and feel it like you were there. Now reach out and grab a silly moment. Step into that moment now and you can even fake laugh, because that turns into real laughter. Now think of an exciting moment in your life.

Imagine you reach into the future and grab a proud moment, something great that is going to happen. Find a beautiful moment from the future, bring it to your heart and say yes. Now stack all those feelings together and bring it in. Feel it, build all the joy, energy, and excitement and really feel it! Breathe it and feel it. It's in you, you don't have to fake it. Everything you want in your future, you've already experienced. But if you don't stack it inside yourself, the world will stack it negatively.

I want you to think of that unfinished business and finish this sentence from your heart. Say "All I need to remember, and do in that situation, all I need to focus on is X" and your heart has the answer. What did you remember in that instant? What did you resolve?

Garrett J. White

In a few hours you'll go home and you'll be alone. There's no motivating, or exciting experience there. It's a darkness on the backside of creation. Every person who built something has walked through this pit of darkness.

When it's not working, and you are against yourself in that space, there's a voice you will hear. You can't state your way out of darkness. There's only one force and power to awaken in the darkness, that voice is not mine, Tony's or yours. It's a place of submission because God gave you that vision.

There's a truth that came into my life and it was the voice of God. That voice is calling me to become this new identity. This requires it to go deep into you and decide whether you choose to live or die. To lose yourself. To the opinions of social media? No. It's the man or woman in the arena. But in that place there's one mistake we make. We are unwilling to submit that everything you had created had come from God.

There's a decision you are going to have to make. Will you let go of your way? Permission must be granted by you first to open up to the glory and grace of God. People look for it in motivation but it won't last. You will temporarily pull yourself out only to fall back again. God cannot step into your world in a mountain of lies. Can you stand in truth?

You want to build a funnel? It's not hard. What's hard is submitting to the calling. When Russell built ClickFunnels I was the 32nd user and I didn't know how it would work. When I accepted the call from God to go, I knew what it would require. It was war with myself, with my wife, with my life. I put myself into a position to believe.

This is the stillness where he finds you. There's just you and a choice. In ten years, the founders of this company have walked in darkness to get to this point. The light is a gift. Russell and Todd didn't know that launching ClickFunnels would help so many people. I didn't know that signing up would be the step I needed. To be great at marketing? No this is what was required to end the suicides and divorces.

You have to choose. Many of you are going to leave and nothing will change. Until you surrender. The community that was built here was built by God. There's one truth behind this community. A knowingness in their soul that they were called to this. How many of you know you have been called to speak God's truth into the world?

Russell and Todd made a decision to turn on the light, and this became the consequence. Everyone's lights are on. You have a moment in time to make a decision. I didn't see this book I wrote, but what I saw was a moment when I made a decision. There was a covenant between me and God and I said I'm going to do what I was asked to do.

For years I messed it up because I couldn't understand where the actual power to create was coming from. Close your eyes for a moment. Take a deep breath in and release. Do it again. As you breathe in you are going to hold it at the top and release it when I say move.

I'm going to ask a question: Are you called by God to lead?

Now take a deep breath in and release. Open your eyes.

Know that you will be tested in your money, your marriage, with your body, your children and by life. And there is a decision that must be made - no different by Noah, Moses, Abraham, Matthew, Luke and John. The one characteristic of those who lead is they are not afraid of the dark. But you can use the tools Tony taught you to put you in a state.

This energy is the energy of creation. And this knowing can only come from knowing God. It's a willingness to become something new by dying. It's an awakening movement.

Even if you don't accept or believe it, it's what is activating transformation in your life every time you surrender. Two years ago I put my marriage on the line. Ladies you must be willing to do the hard win with your man. So I'd like my wife, Danielle to share.

Danielle White

I think that the message is sharing your truth and as a woman I think we don't often share our feelings. We don't think that any guidance we can give our men will be helpful. I understood I'd be doing our family a disservice if I didn't share what I was feeling. We had bought our dream house in CA and it was amazing. Our 4 kids were there and for a year I was telling myself I should be happy and there was a piece of me that felt like I was dying.

I came to Garrett saying I didn't care about the cars, or the house and I felt like I'd lost my sense of purpose. In this honesty we were able to course correct. It's so important to share your truth and be honest as often as you can.

We really worked on our marriage and came back together. Two months ago we were having dinner and I didn't know if I could share this truth. I said I was willing to give up the house. I felt this calling from God telling me it's not the cars, or the money, and I needed to listen. All of you will be blessed with abundance if you listen to that voice. He'll test you along the way.

So two months ago, we sold my company and moved to Miami for a fresh start. There's no end, there's only a rebirth.

Garrett J. White
1. Wake up
2. Take a knee, be honest about where you are and what you desire

You are required to start doing things, like be in Prime Movers. We were required to move to Miami. There's things that God keeps asking you to do to attain a life that's so much bigger that you don't look at it as a sacrifice. It feels like you sacrificed but when it's greater here it was simply a surrender to attain something more.

The last stage is a game of freedom, to be free to create. Free of our lives and free of our willingness to do it our way. His way is faster, our way is slower. Our ability to create will expand.

I got a text from Russell and felt their pain at running this company. How many of you are aware that it takes a mountain of effort to put events like this on? If your life has been radically altered by this community, stand up.

Can your two co-founders of ClickFunnels Russell and Todd come on the stage? This is what you did. You kept believing and you let me be the craziest variable of all, to come here and to help. And you kept leading from the front.

Now comes the statement, We love you. For some of you, you are new. I'm old and I've been here for ten years and I've watched the impact they have made. You need to say it from the heart.

Feel the love, you did great. You did this for ten years and we exist in this game because of you.

I saw something in these guys 10 years ago. I followed Russell and Todd for 10 years. We followed your vision and that vision had a season. This is the room you changed and for myself I'm grateful.

Bonus: Day With Dan Kennedy

Dan Kennedy & Russell Brunson

Dan - There's very little difference in any business. We have to attract people to the business, sort them out and if we bring them in as leads, we have to convert them to a sales opportunity. A sale then has to be made, and that's the same with every business. Some have harder economics, with more expensive acquisition costs.

Everyone is quick to discredit methodology when they haven't seen it defined to their business. Most people will answer that question with their deliverables. They will say they have an ecommerce site, or they have a shoe store for example. That causes them to think their business is different and it won't apply to them. If they think of themself as being in the marketing business with a deliverable, then they get closer to thinking that all businesses are the same.

In Vegas, they'll go to a restaurant and have a great time and will never translate what they are experiencing to their business because it's different. Disney does it with no adult shows and no gambling and they still beat Vegas in getting the greatest dollars per day per person.

Russell - if you are in a market where you are trying to disrupt it, like when we first built ClickFunnels, during that time I'd listen to you for hours each day. I wanted you in mind talking me through it while we were building ClickFunnels. The first question I want to lead with is: it's easy to see the tip of the iceberg but what are the other things you need to disrupt the market?

Dan - when you look at a business category you typically only see the tip of the iceberg. If you are already in it, you only see your methodology. Technical advancement for the Amish is very slow because they tend to only see each other.

You only see the top of what's visible to the naked eye and you hear what's being said at that level. What's not being said is what's most important in disrupting and leapfrogging in a market.

In many markets, it's built around personality. Most established markets have an organized ruling class - a leadership that has a book of rules for its purpose to maintain their position and the status quo. If there's money and a good number of people involved, there will be an establishment created with rules.

Who is on the home owners committee? There are a bunch of petty people who have no authority anywhere else so they get to make up rules and defend those rules forever. When I started speaking in 1978, I joined the National Speakers Association which has 4,000 members. That's enough to cause this phenomena with a group of people that creates rules on how the business is supposed to be done. In most cases, many rules are created to discourage new competition.

They can't admit that a newcomer has a better way. If you do something differently and more successfully, they have to say they should have figured it out. Instead they become violently defensive about their rules. There is a segment of the market that is already quietly grumbling to themselves and are saying in their self talk or maybe to their spouse, that this does not compute. But they feel like they are the only ones. So they play along and are waiting for someone to come along and say what they are thinking.

Most people know about Luther and the Catholic church. His big thing had to deal with buying indulgences. At the time you could pay for your sin to be okay. And everyone went along with this, until he said this does not compute. So there's a bunch of people always waiting for that and I found the opportunity in the speaker community.

As an example, almost every association has awards that theoretically are designed to encourage behavior to make you more successful. At the NSA you had to have 100 fee paid speaking engagements from 100 different clients in order to apply to get your pin. If you are really good and a corporation invites you back 10 times, that doesn't count. So the way to win the award is to be so bad that no one wants to use you twice.

I did one gig and I entered into a contract to do 20 more. Really, their whole dogma was that way. In the chiropractic industry, when we disrupted it with pre-pay, I was involved in this wave. The professional establishment went nuts and said you can't do that.

If you watch Shark Tank, they have a particular built-in bias about bringing in new products to market, which causes them to give bad advice because they really don't understand direct response.

So this is a dangerous thing, but there's also the opportunity because there's people doubting them as they don't want to be the odd man out. They keep saying to themselves "there has to be a better way".

Russell - Daymond John is the only shark I know that uses ClickFunnels for shark tank deals.

Dan - People can be really smart but narrow and people like to repeat what has worked for them but it causes them to block out other ways of doing things and opportunities.

Russell - After we understand the markets, how do we understand what we need to be the disruptors?

Dan - your opportunities to be explosive grows the more entrenched the business is, because the dissatisfaction is growing. Their willingness to hear a new and better way after 10 years of oppression is greater than it was after 3 years.

That's a marker of opportunity. Where the dogma seems silly to you, that's good. They are intimidated by being in the club and having no one else say it. The red cap phenomena of the moment is happening in the 2nd term because people's dissatisfaction was growing and a bigger number of people were ready to hear certain things.

The more dogmatic the rules of the road are, the bigger your opportunity. Lawyers at one time were not allowed to advertise and it became a free speech issue. One guy asked why does everyone else have a right to advertise and we don't. A few others said that it didn't make sense.

So the more entrenched it is, the better because when you break that dam, it's profound. The last thing you look for is any sign at all of some little breakout group, where someone is objecting to the way things are done in this business.

The people that are attracted to you because of that are more rapid than normal customers, because they have been blocked in a box, but have not been able to knock it apart. But you come along and give them permission to knock it apart and they get excited.

Russell - How do you identify these things?

Dan - You need to identify your position because you are going to be against some portion of the dogma and the rules of the road. You start to craft your radical position. You need a radical statement about what's going on. In the NSA, the first time I delivered it, I did a free one day seminar the day before the NSA convention. I probably had 300-350 people there and I told them that speaking is not a business. At best it's a good job, but if you get sick you don't get paid and you can never stop showing up. Plus you have a lot of expenses. So some people got mad and walked out but others said it made sense.

You didn't have any customers, you had gigs. You didn't have any recurring revenue. If you have a shoe store, you get a day off and someone is still going to come in and buy shoes.

This was as radical as you could get at the time. At the time, selling from the stage wasn't really done. The people who did it were celebrated to their face but the NSA still had a fee based model.

This is your radical big idea, which in my case, was that it's not a business. The second thing is your position where you are taking on the wise elders, the authority, the church, or the board where what they are saying is all wrong. I did a lot more work with the sales audience in my early years and if you read the No BS Sales Success book I told salespeople that their sales managers were idiots.

The suits in a big company were basically bean counters. In a small company, the sales manager is detrimental to you because he tells you what he did, which is to dial more phone numbers and sales is about numbers.

I didn't get invited back, but there were a lot of customers. They were the first ones in the back to buy and they are now glued to you because you have spoken the truth. They knew it, but no one said anything about it.

The third thing is what your man on the white horse position is going to be because you have to ride to the rescue. You can't bluff anything and walk out. You have to have a man on a white horse position so that now that I have shown you that these people, out of ignorance are selling you a bad plan, and you are working a really bad plan, I have the alternative and I will happily lead you to the land of milk and honey.

So you have to figure out those 3 things and advertise them.

There's two guys who are basically the options trading guys. They are running a free book campaign now and their whole argument is "don't buy stocks" and that you should only buy options. Then they show you the math difference. So they have a radical idea where everyone is glued to the stock market and they have the white horse plan. You can make more money on one trade than you can do with stocks all year.

With pre-pay, if you are paying a large amount of money you'll show up for your appointments and it's better for the patients because they tend to do the stuff at home that they need to. I have a client who has sellmoreimplants.com, and it's the same as the options trading argument.

Years ago I started to write my first book. Nowadays, the big gatekeepers are not around as much. Back then, there was a hierarchy to get your book published. You had to do a big proposal, and a competitive title analysis, then find an agent, submit packages to the agents and beg them to get someone to accept you. If you were lucky you'd get a deal for little or no advance. You might establish a good enough record that you could get another book published.

This sounded very slow to me. So I thought, why don't I just go see the publishers because I'm a sales guy. But I was told you can't do that.

At the big book expo, I went and most of the publishers had the presidents there in a booth for the five days of the show. So I door hopped essentially, talking about my book and I got a deal. Afterwards, my agent at the time couldn't believe that it happened.

I went to another event for fiction and was told the same thing about having to get an agent. I was thinking that this was a bucket list item for me and it was a bad plan. There was a guy who had about 30 mystery novels published, and he's right in my backyard. I had my nonfiction agent figure out how many books he was selling and I know now what his annual income is. So I took a shortcut.

I told him I'd like to do a book for him, I can provide a setting you haven't used yet and I will educate you. I told him I wanted a second chair to learn and I'd write him a check for $X which was roughly twice what he was making for writing his next book. Of course he took it, and we ended up doing two books together.

Most of this happens often, and pretty soon it's the religion of that business where no opportunity for independent thought exists, until you trigger the unhappy natives who are living in the system and are privately questioning it.

Russell - you said ⅓ of the people are feeling that way but are not doing anything. How do you not have the fear to step up?

Dan - The fear is real and you do have to be prepared for the backlash that will come. In most cases, they are unlikely to crucify you but there are people who come close to that.

The better at this you are, the bigger the backlash will be. Some of it is psycho-emotion and you have to not care about the critics. When I was doing a lot of speaking, I tried to get some people to get up and leave. You knew you were in a place where no one was missing your point. You have to not care about any of that and people tend to obsess about it.

They may get complaint letters, and other than when they've been funny, I don't think anyone has shown me one in 3 years. Now you are getting them. I had to be okay with being there for 3 days and seeing people cluster to avoid me or talk amongst themselves.

You do have to prepare those around you. Your family and your staff is going to hear about it and they have to be immunized to it. You have to do your own opposition research and you want to know what is in your past that can be attacked for whatever reason. Most people have at least a few things.

I got a lot of heat over the years where people were saying I'm only in it for the money. But businesses are about profit and in many cases you can preempt it by teaching and disclosing. Transparency makes a lot of personal attacks impossible. I never tried to hide my bankruptcy and I knew if I tried to hide it, it would bite me at the worst possible time. So you might as well tell it and make it funny.

You can pre-empt it by telling what your critics are going to say about it. In one of my first businesses, I quickly discovered that they were going to tell people they joined Amway. Whoever they told it to, was instantly on a mission to rescue them by selling them out.

The evening ended with a talk about the 5 things you will hear and here are the facts. Then we had a cassette tape which was essentially the same talk titled "The 5 Ways People Will Destroy Your Dreams."

I was thrown out of the NSA for an ethics violation which was rescinded with a printed apology in the newsletter. Think about how many thought leaders were trying to kill the chiropractor idea of pre-pay.

The media will also attack you. In the chiropractor world, they had a newspaper and they went after us every week. It was a pretty heavy hatchet job. But for five years, even though the press was negative, we used "As Seen on 60 Minutes" and "As Seen on CBS" in our advertising.

With your big, radical idea you have to be able to put that across in a big way. We would take the Atkins weight loss products, and Dr. Atkins started the anti-carb diet, saying the food pyramid is wrong. The original Atkins diet is a radical big idea attacked by pretty much the entire medical establishment. That happens a lot.

When they created Superman, you needed supervillains to go along with the super heroes. That's the same for all of us who want to take this position. Next, it needs to make itself visible. You've got to be in physical locations, and you've got to be able to do something a little dramatic in the way you present this stuff.

You want to get it right when you do it. Where you have a situation where you gather all these people, and it's the only association for what it is. Some people are questioning privately what they are being told, and when that erupts everything changes.

The Trump rallies in and of themselves persuade some people because there's exit interviews. They go pre-determined to hate it, but then they see all these people and think how can all these people be crazy? Then you start to talk to them and some of them are rational. Some of them are lawyers and doctors. So if you are going to start, you need to start big.

I had three coach buses that had signs on them for free transportation. I also had a big billboard saying "Dan Kennedy and NSA welcome you to Phoenix". They are almost asking for it in many of these markets because they are enforcing dumb or self-serving things from the top down.

You have to be willing to not be welcomed, at least for a while. You have to be very results oriented, but you want the opposition too, visibly and vocally.

Opposition is the quickest way to attract attention. Historically there was a multi level marketing business that was later outlawed as a pyramid scheme. The laws didn't exist at the time. There was a cosmetics and motivational company which predates the internet, so there was no cheap media.

You bought your $30 kit and you only made money when something sells. All of sudden you could recruit 4 people and make $1,000. They discovered inventory loading and because he took all the attacks, it brought more attention to him.

When we came to town to do a meeting, they came to see what this horrible person was all about. Three hours later, they were signed up. The opposition drove the attendance.

When he wrote a book about it, he leaned into this everywhere he could. There's no better way to get attention than the opposition screaming about you all the time, because there's curiosity.

There was a pretty famous speaker, where he said "I'll deny this if you talk about it, but I'm famous and I'm not making any money and I can't figure it out". He wanted to see me but I had to promise not to tell anyone. That's how high the opposition was in his immediate peer group. The opposition is helpful and responds to it the right way.

Fisher Investments had a position against the annuities. They went to the TV stations and ran a campaign. I had an ad refused and we printed it up saying it was the ad that they refused to run, so here it is. We went to a hotel and asked the people to leave it in all of the rooms which were having the convention. The screaming went off for a year afterwards.

I said no one told us that I couldn't put these things in the room. They turned this into an open feud and got on the stage talking about it. The curiosity goes through the roof now. Maybe there's something there and maybe this guy knows something because they are so afraid of him.

For a while there was a website called DanKennedyIsAThief.com run by a few ex-members and a guy I threw out of a seminar. They made a project out of this. That's maybe the bad side of this but the good thing is you have access to all of this too. When there's a lot of opposition to you, you have to have an online presence.

Trump's kid ran a part of the campaign this time and they were everywhere. So someone hears a lot of bad stuff and they decide to take a look. Wherever their impulse is, you want to be there to accommodate it. If their impulse is to go to Amazon and see if they have a book, you want to have a book available. It almost doesn't matter if the noise is good or bad.

When the rest of the people find a truth tower and the man on the white horse, he is a better customer. That means a bunch of things such as conversion percentages.

Russell - Do you recommend anything specific for those things?

Dan - It's pretty formulaic. If you think about the MLM industry or the diet industry with Atkins, and you pick a category, there's a lot of models. That history is all there all the way back to the bookstore model. There's these models in every category and then there's the instruction angles for the aftermath. Read Eric Hoffer's book - The True

Believer. So there's no shortage of things to look at, understand what each part loves and replicate.

The early disruptors of agency models in advertising, all wrote a book exploiting those and their radical ideals. Ogilvy was very contrary to traditional advertising at the time. Most advertising at the time was basically brand advertising and didn't have more than a logo and picture of a building, and there's your ad. Ogilvy wore a cape and drove a Rolls Royce. He used to park this thing right in front of his office.

So you'll almost always find a book, or now a podcast or YouTube channel. It allows people to find you but to get people to look, you have to stir up where people already are.

Jay Abraham used an ad which the headline was "Who is this man and why is he saying these terrible things in your business?" Over time, opposition arose and it worked well. In today's world, an ad like that would be more productive because it's easy to find him and get cooked in his environment.

Each media always creates a spinoff and if you don't capture it, you lose it. When you have opposition to you being voiced, that drives traffic and as long as you are there to get it and carry that message forward, you benefit from all of the acquisition. It takes a lot longer to get famous by getting famous than to get famous by getting infamous. The more places you are, the more you benefit because people will look you up in different places. Like in this last round, Trump was everywhere and you couldn't avoid it.

I've always gone out of my way to trigger the opposition. If you take any No B.S. book, they all have this early hook and there is an establishment. There's a thing that's attacked then a system that is offered to you.

Russell - I remember there was an ad that showed 5 star Amazon reviews for the book and also a 1 star review and the ad said "This book should be banned and both of them are right."

Dan - Years ago the Catholic church put out a list of movies you shouldn't watch and they were driving a whole bunch of people to see these movies. They banned The Exorcist when it came out, which was basically a junk horror film that I think would have died at the box office if the church hadn't made such a big stink about it. This is like your parents telling you not to read a book. You'll want to read the book now.

The book was about scandals in a small town. It was fiction but based on real people. So it was the housewife's hidden book of the year. It was a contemporary phenomenon like 50 Shades of Gray at the time, which is a very funny book. So this book was hidden and it took me about a day to find it.

This is the opposite of being dominated by disapproval. I think that a third of what Trump is doing is things like this, mostly to entertain himself and to create another blast to create conversation. It's amazing to me how the media always bites.

I wonder, when it goes through his head, if he says to himself "this will be fun". There's a lot of it and it accumulates and it's actually magnetic.

You just have to not care about the disapproval and it's so contrary. We see this model but you don't see it currently used because if everyone used it, it would disintegrate. Most business people are hypersensitive to any disapproval and they are getting an exercise in futility and are seeking no disapproval.

You are never going to be the talk of the town because of that. If that worked in 2016, Jeb Bush would be president. But there was nothing to really get excited about

This is contrary to the way we are taught to behave, from childhood on up. If you are the media for a time, the two highest paid broadcasters were Rush Limbaugh & Howard Stern. They had two diverse audiences and not a lot in common, other than the fact that they said triggering things which caused people to be curious. Howard has some fans but not a lot and Limbaugh didn't have any liberal fans.

If you are looking for a model you are looking at not being a pleasant morning radio AM host, where they do the weather, traffic and talk about events. They are never going to move up the media ladder and the model is Stern and Limbaugh. You would go back from Howard on day one, and forward to see what they did if you wanted to become a top 10 radio personality.

With Joe Rogan's model, all of his secrets are visible. One of the things he does is saying controversial things and he has people on his show, who are disapproved of. He really helped Trump and Trump helped him as there was a whole new audience in both directions. That tells you that, if you are using a podcast, make sure you have people on it that offend you. There's no point in having someone that everyone will forget.

One of the things with this model is "radical with radical", not only positive with negative because you want to be talked about.

Dan Kennedy and Marty Fort

Marty - Who has competition and saturation in your market? What do we need in place to capture the attention in the marketplace?

Dan - an apparently saturated market where there are a lot of people ahead of you, like everything else, is the proverbial double sided coin. So if there's nearly no one there, that seems like an advantage but it also means no one has been taught to respond to lead generation and buy.

When you go into a market where there's already a lot, the good news is first, they have already taught people how to respond. I have two clients where we do a lot of marketing in dentistry. There are a lot of consultants, coaches and conferences. Every dentist has already learned how to respond.

The dentist has already done what we are asking him to do. Come to this webinar and here's what you will find out. That's the good news. The even better news is the way market saturation occurs and is copycatting. They present themselves as clones. Also, a lot of the competitors were customers, students or members of the others ones. This is all great if you figure out the gap to present yourself that is profoundly different and against.

For the most part they don't know how to deal with the arrival of the radical heretic. With each generation, they get dumber and dumber and don't know how to respond. Combine that with the profound likelihood that your marketplace has a percentage of restless natives, so when you arrive very differently and you present that way, it works even better when there's a lot of look- alike competition.

The big key to know you are on the right track is if a big reaction from the established leaders is "How dare he say that" about this, us or them, etc. Because that's a binary move. So it repels but it's also very attractive to restless natives and there's a certain level of respect that goes to the person who says what no one else will.

I mentioned Rush Limbaugh and he was in the permission slip business. Stern gave a 28 year old permission to act like a 14 year old in the locker room. Limbaugh gave a permission slip to think and talk like they were already doing with their buddies.

Hefner is a great model for this as well. In its time, Playboy was this business model because the idea of non-reproductive, recreational sex was very radical at the time and was opposed by all the religious leaders. If you study his building of the business, you'll see how he did it in the way we talked about earlier.

Marty - Once we learned all this stuff, how do we capture that attention?

Dan - Conversion is actually a religious word, where you convert to a way of thought, a way of life. Conversion is not just making a sale, you want conversion that makes a relationship and a fan.

This is a market matched to best reach to media. The tighter the match, the better. There's paid media and many don't do that enough or are too cheap about it. Then there's borrowed media and in many cases you can invade because a lot of tribe leaders and media owners are lazy. They are overwhelmed because of the insatiable appetite for content.

They often step in by providing non-competitors reinforcing content, which tribe leaders will gladly use and you are now borrowing their medium.

There's owned media which is your own. You need to be able to move people from all the media to yours and have them stay there.

If you leave your interaction with only Facebook for example they can decide you don't have that access anymore. You want your media platform because it lets you turn back around and borrow other people's media.

Then there's earned media which is the greatest expansion of successful media, although it's not new. For example, Houdini made his mark with earned media and his own. He went from city to city, inviting the media to watch him do his tricks and that got media everywhere he went. He also might be one of the first to produce his own fake documentary. He made a newsreel about himself and gave it to the media for free.

Years later in the get rich in real estate genre, this one guy would take someone and no matter their talent, he would find a good investment for them with no money down.

What is now the Stratosphere was originally Vegas World. It was bought years ago and it was a one story, slot machine only place. He was in that dead zone between the end of the strip and downtown. Bob Stupak had a popular court case which started him doing earned media. He was on 60 Minutes once where he played poker against a robot and beat it. So he was very much into getting free media through controversial ways.

He had no debt, and built one floor at a time because he got pre-paid vacation packages and the place was always under construction. The rooms were made with cheap materials and he compensated it by giving them a bunch of stuff. At 2 am, a marching band would appear and he'd give out free hot dogs. He was a great promoter and was constantly coming up with ideas.

Earned media is the last kind on the list and you really want it all. You want to be the news of the day and above the fold. You pump content out to spark this reaction "How dare he say that". If you get that a lot, you get all this media opportunity.

Marty - How do we keep this momentum building?

Dan - The obvious strategy is you have got to produce. In Bob's case, that hotel had to produce for its guests, what they considered to be a great experience. Most people there bought a $399 package in advance. It was really about the ordinary Joe having the experience of a high roller. And he delivered an experience that people really liked.

He gave free drinks away, there was always entertainment, there was a buffet, it was cramped so it always seemed like it was packed. There were prizes and gifts and people had a ball. If you were going to take on a market, and you are not the only one with the truth serum, you better deliver once you get someone inside your walls. There needs to be visible proof that helps the doubter feel reassured.

Another one is your associations and your cast of characters and you really want two. You want a couple of other radicals if you can, then you also want the opposite of what you are - a reassuring, respected normal person.

When Herbalife was under attack and in pretty serious financial trouble, the reaction was that it can't be that bad because they have Jim Rohn. In my NSA experience, up against a lot of opposition and criticism, I mentored its young president at the time who was the star of the association. Everyone loved him and we did some seminars, where our company took over the product of his audience cassette program. It was worth every penny because the formula is the same. How can this company, this guy, this city be as bad if he's with it?

There is no telling how much of the youth vote Trump got this time. It's the same formula. I know that it has the same effect, after talking to some family members. It can't be that bad because I love Elon Musk, and that association factor is very powerful. There's almost no market you'll go into where there are wise people on the backside of their creators who can be rented. It's at the local and national level both.

For many years, in the siding and window replacement industry, it was to go get that retired weather guy. So he's available at a reasonable cost, and now you've got him in your commercials and people make the connection. This company has got to be okay because they have the local weatherman.

Most people know they are being paid but even so, they impute a sense of reassurance and a questioning of any bad they have heard because that person is attached to it.

Marty - How do we keep the momentum without burning out our market and ourselves?

Dan - You won't burn out your market because this model is entertaining. If you want to educate and inform people, you almost always first have to entertain. Therefore, it's very hard to overuse a lot. If you are doing something every day that causes a reaction of "How dare you do that" you will not wear out the market's interest in you.

The first decision that separates people who get results and those who don't is coming to grips with the fact that your deliverables are your business. I don't have time for all that because I'm filling the deliverable. If they default back to that, they don't get it. That guarantees at best, mediocre returns.

That allows you to forcibly ring in the time and energy for deliverability and expand the time and energy to run this model. That's the biggest part of the answer to your dilemma.

Marty - How does this topic apply to Howard Hughes?

Dan - There's a great parallel between Howard Hughes and Elon Musk. He was an aviator, and finished his later years maybe completely crazy. Now instead of investing in the moon, his offshoot was investing in the movies and actresses.

Elvis was on the variety show but because of the controversy in the way he girated they blocked out the lower half on the tv screen. What that does is everyone wants to see, so it was a great media coup.

Marty - In regards to Frank Sinatra, he was going to make his own record label. Would you agree he's an example of this?

Dan - Sinatra went out of his way to pick fights with the media and I think he knew that it reinforced the narrative of Sinatra beyond his music. Again, this was in the Playboy era, so the swinging brat pack bunch was appealing to a lot of fans. Frank was the best business person of any of them, by far and was pretty smart. John Wayne was asked about his acting career and said "I just play John Wayne". To some degree, Sinatra created a persona and sold it as much as he did as a singer.

The parallel there is I would give Sinatra points for understanding that his deliverables were not his business. He never shied from controversy and was a big fan of the civil rights movement. He literally changed Vegas' policy towards black entertainers.
There was a Sinatra narrative that Frank intentionally put out there a lot that had nothing to do with his deliverables.

Marty - Do you have any closing thoughts?

Dan - The momentum of this comes from consistency not from random acts, so if you decide to run this model, the early phase of it is rising up in a market out of nowhere and becoming infamous. But it's not like you are going to do that for 9 months, then you get to stop. If you choose this model, phase 2 is continuing it at least at a maintenance level forevermore. You have to keep rising up with the latest "How dare he do that" actions.

Zig often was asked if he'd like to speak and if he could leave out the evangelical call and he said no. There are some people who are offended and will complain. I said it has to be everywhere you speak, not just here. He said my first purpose is that, so the business consideration is second. He said what I've learned is that the effectiveness of it, which is a relatively small number, is the bargain of the century compared to what it brings me in.

So from a business standpoint it's the smart thing to do. Zig had a multi generational draw to his shows because he was so consistent over the decades. One of the things I've tried to do is be trend or fad orientated. I've tried to be very consistent.

I sat down the other day looking at my faxes and it's amazing to me how consistent I've been. When you pick what you are going to do, how you are going to present yourself to the marketplace, and what game you are going to use, you want to be consistent.

There are people in our business who keep recreating themselves every 3-4 years and many of them run out of gas. I think that consistency is the secret element to long term sustained success.

Dan Kennedy & Darcy Juarez

Dan - Disney's first obligation is to maximize their revenue for shareholders and fill that park. They sell yearly passes at a deep discount plus discounts on other stuff. They discovered that the season passport holders are worth lower amounts compared to the retail buyer so they are doing that program over. They are making things cost extra, adding blackout dates, etc.

I had a conversation about it recently with a longtime season passport holder who was enraged. I asked why they would renew their season pass, and he said because it's Disney. The folks at Disney are choosing in part, who they want in there by their spending value for the days they are there.

The truth about businesses small or large, is your first responsibility is to maximize returns to shareholders. That means that you have to exercise some control over who gets in and who doesn't. You have to discriminate as much as possible.

We did seminars for medical professionals and for whatever reason, it was very hard for us to sell to Asian doctors. I don't know why, I only know what I saw. Increasingly we have a funnel where the middle is hollowed out. Because we don't want more customers that are social workers, we want customers with the willingness and the ability to buy. Ideally you want customers for whom your pricing is not discouraging.

You are picking your customers by merit and by value. You have to be very clear that you have the right to do that. You have a responsibility to decide who you let in.

Darcy - Are there some warnings we need to be aware of when we start to do this?

Dan - Your own attitudes and the attitudes of people around you will interfere. My client makes it brutally clear who they are for and who they are not for.

I noticed in the last two weeks they raised the minimum to a $1 million as to who they will take on as clients. So that tells you that some level of analysis has told them that if they have less than a million, they are not wanted as clients.

No matter how eloquently that is done, there will be people who are outraged, but you need to let them out as gently as you can. There's a place for you but this is not it. Unless you are willing to say, "this is not it" you are going to have business problems because of the inability to pay for your customers

Darcy - If we are new to this, what kind of data do we need to determine who makes our best customers?

Dan - There will be factors - anything from geographic to occupational to color of hair to educational level - there will be biases in common with your best customers or clients. You may very well have that information and not have put it together in a meaningful way.

There is your own information and in many industries there's buyer research that can be bought. There are data scientists who can get that information if you don't want that. Trade associations have a lot of data about Gen Z vs. Gen X vs. Gen Y, so you can get as much information as you can and you continue to refine that.

Then there's the issue of who would you prefer to have as a customer. We're always dealing with two questions - do they have the ability to buy from me at my price? If they do not have it, you try and set up screening which either absolutely keeps them out or discourages them through your messaging.

The second question is their willingness to buy at your prices. Even really rich people may be completely ignorant of the price of X but very cognizant of the price of Y. Even though they have that ability to pay for the price of Y, for whatever reason it brings up trouble for them.

Darcy - I want to shift to the affluent and you have a book that you are releasing in April. Can we talk about quick tips on how we take everything you talked about and how we market to the affluent?

Dan - Very often our measure of success is based on how many transactions we have, how many customers we've got, etc. We don't do anything for ourselves with gross though. Everything that we do for ourselves, we do with net. Net is not necessarily increasing by size. You have to think about 'per customer value' and often marketing to the affluent is the key to more for less. It's the anecdote for this constant need for more customers.

Instead of increasing the number of dental patients, why don't we increase the value of a patient?

Even if they don't experience it personally, there's a spending dollar floating around out there. You can't even land here without a spot. It costs a lot of money to fly one of those private jets. You look at all these planes and when I started flying private, it was not advertised to the general public. That was unheard of at the time.

Nowadays, there's a company called Badger which is like Uber for private jets. You can pick the one you want and you're all set. You shouldn't be able to advertise this on television. If you were doing it, then maybe on Fox and CNN. But they are running this ad on a lot of stations. Recently, they added that if you qualify, you can have your flight for free.

What was bought by this tiny minority, is now being bought by a much bigger minority. What once was only the super-rich did that, now the moderately rich do that. The buyer is up to date on that, but the marketer is not necessarily up to date on that. So it's good to go to places like that. Go to the boat show or a classic car auction. All this money is out there and marketers still have a tendency that they want to show you what's on sale.

It's middle class, what we call mass affluent. It used to be where a lot of stuff was free. This was the dollar buffet because you would come here to gamble and we'd get all this stuff for free. Now, there's nothing for free. Now the buffet here is $85. That's where the market has moved. There's a lot more people with a lot more spending power than there's ever been.

Dan Interviews The Million Dollar Waiter From A Local Restaurant

Dan - Tell us about where you work.

Waiter - There's 18-20 tables, and the average check is $450-$500. The biggest tip I received was $23,000.

Dan - What are you doing differently?

Waiter - When someone comes in the clock is ticking to get their contact information. We send out Valentine's packages which are expensive and time consuming but those checks will be $3,000-$5,000. I don't own the restaurant but I own the relationship.

They know the service will be impeccable and I don't leave until the last person leaves.

Darcy - What is the biggest secret out of everything we discussed today?

Dan - The things that you think would do harm to you in your business actually do you the most good. I'm relatively inaccessible and I have been for a long time. When I had an office, my staff person was very apolitical. We would get calls from time to time where they would want to talk to me. Our standard answer was that they had to put a memo together about what they wanted to talk to me about and fax it in.

I would call every day and make myself available to her, and she said someone had called three times and was very annoyed. His name was Carl and I took his number and after I got the fax about what he wanted to talk about.

People are like cats, they can't stand being in a room with a closed door - it drives them nuts. Often the things that you think would do you harm, end up doing you the most good.

Martin collects the contact information of everyone who comes into the business because he does direct follow up with them. And he sends these goofy giant greeting cards that are relevant to the person. He's made shock and awe packages and you might think, a really important person would not want their privacy invaded, but the opposite is true.

When you have a thought on your own, or more likely a thought from a spouse or staff member who reacts to it negatively, that's a really good reason to do it.

Made in the USA
Las Vegas, NV
18 March 2025

f7bb4b20-20a2-4d71-b1c4-1ab52cc06348R01